D0065682

110
÷US
6.95

The AMERICAN HERITAGE GUIDE TO Antiques

ℳ AMERICAN HERITAGE

GUIDE TO
⌐Antiques

by MARY DURANT

AMERICAN HERITAGE PRESS, NEW YORK

A Subsidiary of McGraw-Hill

Title pages: The Thomas Hancock house, a superb example of Georgian architecture in America, was built on Beacon Hill in Boston 1737–40 and razed in the 1860's.

ART DIRECTOR: Murray Belsky
EDITOR: Beverley Hilowitz
PRODUCTION SUPERVISOR: Thomas C. Partis
ASSISTANT ART DIRECTOR: Wayne Young
DRAWINGS: Helen Disbrow, Joseph Papin, Ray Porter, Cal Sacks, Chas. B. Slackman

Library of Congress Catalog Card No.: 72-111653
SBN: 8281-0088-8 (paper)
       8281-0087-X (cloth)

Introduction

It was not until the closing years of the last century that Americans, to their surprise and delight, discovered American antiques. In 1878, *Godey's Lady's Book* reported to its readers that antiques were, in fact, "the latest mania among fashionable people." This comment was corroborated in the 1880's by a contemporary art critic who wrote that "all this resuscitation of old furniture" had actually begun in Boston among a "circle of rich, cultivated people." The craze, it was further explained, had worked down to a wider circle of people, who — while not blessed with large incomes — were nonetheless blessed with "natural good taste," and the New England countryside was being "scoured by young couples in chaises on the trail of old sideboards and brass andirons." In 1888, the *Ladies' Home Journal* announced its approval of American antiques, declaring that "nice old-fashioned chairs . . . make a parlor look very cozy and old-timey."

A large part of this enthusiasm, of course, was triggered by the centennial celebrations and the Centennial Exhibition held at Philadelphia in 1876, where one of the most popular exhibits was the New England Farmer's Home. Its rooms were furnished with heirlooms contributed by New Englanders, including such historic pieces as the Fuller cradle brought over on the *Mayflower*, a chair originally made for Governor Endicott of the Massachusetts Bay colony, John Alden's desk, and an ancient spinning wheel from Plymouth, upon which one of the guide books happily romanticized: "This spinning wheel may be the very one that was so deftly whirled by Priscilla, the Puritan maid, that poor John Alden could find no way out of the web she wove about him." The building itself was a one-story log cabin, quite likely the first such historic restoration in the United States. No matter that log cabins were a form of construction introduced by Swedish settlers in the Delaware Valley and quite unknown to the New England colonists—"everything in the household had the ripe flavor of antiquity." And the flavor of antiquity was suddenly à la mode.

Early American houses became fashionable purchases to be restored and refurbished. "Unspoiled" colonial towns became fashionable summer resorts. In Plymouth, as a landmark for the rising tide of tourists, the town fathers enshrined Plymouth Rock under a stone canopy. Statues and monuments on historic themes were unveiled throughout the country — *The Puritan* in Springfield, Massachusetts, *The Minute Man* in Concord, *Nathan Hale* in New York City, to name but a few. As an interesting footnote, it was this new awareness of the historic past that inspired the founding (in the 1890's) of such organizations as the Daughters of the American Revolution, the Society of Colonial Wars, the Society of Mayflower Descendants, and so forth. Meanwhile, American furniture manufacturers were also well aware of the new trend. Some, to fill the demand for good reproductions, made conscientious copies of early styles—from the Jacobean patterns of the 1600's to pre-Civil War fashions in Sheraton and Hepplewhite patterns, all of them enticingly advertised under such headings as "The Furniture of Our Forefathers." Other manufacturers, swept up a random assortment of motifs—Gothic, Empire, Chippendale, a leg here, an arm there—scrambled them together and labeled the product "colonial." Typical of such concoctions was The Old Flax Spinning Wheel Chair advertised in 1886 as a beautiful wedding or birthday present, the back of the chair wheel-shaped and clearly intended to evoke the ever-popular shade of Priscilla Alden. But "colonial-style" concoctions, as we well know, are still on the market today.

The point is, antiques had been discovered. They had arrived to stay. And the mania, as *Godey's* called it almost a century ago, is yet upon us. Ardent collectors still scour the countryside and hurry to local auctions in search of treasures. The buying and selling of antiques has become big business. The study of antiques has become a matter of exacting research and diligent scholarship. Galleries and museums are devoted solely to the exhibition of antiques. Indeed, whole towns have been restored in order to exhibit antiques and the way of life that accompanied them—Colonial Williamsburg in Virginia, Old Sturbridge Village in Massachusetts, Greenfield Village in Michigan.

This book is designed to offer a ready reference to the rich and varied world of American antiques. Wherever possible the historic background has been given, because no furniture fashions—or fashions in glass, silver, or ceramics, for that matter—ever sprang full-blown into vogue. All such styles are a blend of earlier trends and past traditions, borrowed and re-expressed to create "new" styles. A number of imports are listed, particularly in chinaware, because they were as much a part of furnishings and decor of their day as were objects of domestic manufacture. The three opening essays on the techniques used by silversmiths, cabinetmakers, and glassmakers are reprinted from the *American Heritage History of Colonial Antiques* and offer a comprehensive picture of the skilled hand-craftsmanship practiced by American artisans in the years preceding the mass-production factory methods introduced in the 1800's.

Mary Durant

Colonial Crafts

The Art
and Mystery
of a
Goldsmith

The colonial silversmith fashioned his wares by practices and techniques that were ages old; methods that account in good measure for the special character of antique silver, quite aside from the interest and the merit of its design.

British America produced virtually no silver or gold and the craftsman was obliged to use coins and miscellaneous pieces of metal, often of questionable fineness. These he melted down and refined, with reference to a touchstone, to an acceptable standard of purity. Pure silver is relatively soft and for practical use it must be toughened with other metals, chiefly copper, as an alloy. Long before the first American colonies were founded, England had established a standard of quality, known as sterling, that required all silverwork, including coin of the realm, to contain 92.5 per cent pure silver. (To this day the hallmarks on English silver guarantee, among other things, that the standard has been maintained.) Such regulations did not extend to colonial work; the only pledge of quality in early America was the mark of the individual maker and, to be sure, his reputation. Many colonial smiths actually warranted their wares "as good as Sterling."

Almost all the hollow ware produced in the colonies—the bulk of production —was hammered up on anvils from solid, seamless sheets of metal, a process called "raising." First, the silversmith cast his refined, molten metal into a solid form. This, in turn, was hammered into a flat, smooth sheet of the required gauge—generally thicker than that of most modern silverware. On this, with a pair of compasses, he measured a series of concentric circles which he cut out of the sheet with saws or shears. (The cen-

tering mark left by the point of the compass can be seen on the base of an old tankard or bowl.) Since the metal spread in the making, the diameter of this disk was somewhat less than the combined base and height of the piece to be finished.

As a start to the raising process, the disk was placed over one of various-sized, shallow hollows in a wooden sinking block and repeatedly struck with blows of a mallet or hammer in a continuous spiral toward the perimeter, leaving the central area for the base of the form. The piece was then transferred to the first of a series of raising anvils, of different sizes and shapes, and

on these hammered into its final form. As one can still witness at Colonial

Williamsburg and other places where the craft has been revived, or where it has survived, this hammering procedure calls for muscle, skill, and patience.

To complete the raising it was often necessary to resort to a fluted T-shaped anvil, crimping the piece in order to

equalize the stresses set up in the metal by repeated hammering and to prevent it from splitting. Then, changing both anvil and hammer, the smith carefully

smoothed out those creases, always working from bottom to top to bring the piece gradually closer to its final shape. By successive maneuvers of this sort, the use of hammers of different sorts and anvils—or stakes, held in a vise—of different contours that could reach inside the vessel, almost any curved or straight surface could be contrived. To of the iron with a hammer, the smith could transmit the percussion by reciprocal action along the bar to the inside and create an embossed, or *repoussé*, pattern on the surface. The patterns were given greater definition by being indented from the outside with chasing punches that did not cut into the metal but that did sharpen the outlines of the various ornamental elements—(the piece was filled with pitch so that its shape would not be distorted in the process).

reach far inside a deep vessel in order to create a raised pattern on the exterior, a snarling iron was used—a Z-shaped iron, one end of which could be inserted inside the form. By striking the outside

For other kinds of decoration, such as coats of arms, initials, and inscriptions, a graver was used; this actually cut away the surface of the silver and produced a thin, sharp-edged channel. Many colonial silversmiths were accomplished engravers.

To provide a piece of hollow ware with moldings at the lip or base, a strip

of metal was drawn a number of times through the opening between two dies

on a drawing bench. The opening provided the profile of the molding, and with each drawing it was narrowed until the desired thickness was achieved.

These finished moldings often faithfully reproduced, on a tiny scale, the contours of those used in monumental architecture.

The uneven marks left by the raising hammers were smoothed out by further blows from a planishing hammer, and at the end of these procedures, by being rubbed with a pumice stone, and finally

by being polished with a burnishing tool. From time to time, throughout the various steps in its making, the piece had to be annealed, or reheated, over a charcoal fire to keep it malleable. In the course of this operation, oxygen in the

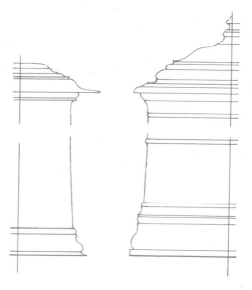

air united with the copper of the alloy to form a thin film of gray or bluish oxide. Neither this so-called fire skin nor all the evidences of hammering were eliminated in the polishing of the metal. The unevenness of the surface and its warm color are two attractive qualities of old silverwork that has not been buffed down by modern methods.

Workers
in
Wood

Those skilled woodworkers, so sorely needed at the beginnings of settlement in America to "make strong ware for the use of the countrie," had arrived in good numbers before the end of the seventeenth century—and they were doing a thriving business. Along with the "ingenious Carpenter" and the "cunning Joyner" called for in William Wood's summons of 1634, there were also "Cabenett Makers" listed as working in various colonies by the 1680's and others who specialized in making chairs. In some respects the problems and practices of these various types of artisans overlapped. The wood they used for surfaces that would show had to be smoothed down from rough, pit-sawn boards before it could be properly handled. For this purpose and for shap-

ing moldings of different contours a variety of planes were required—tools

which, aside from their iron blades, were usually made of maple by the woodworker himself. Some molding

The increasing use of wood-turning lathes late in the seventeenth century resulted, then and later, in a profusion

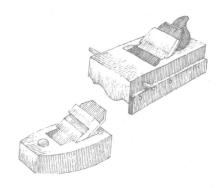

planes were so large they had to be towed with a rope by an apprentice while the master craftsman pushed and steadied the instrument on its way. In 1759 George Washington ordered a long list of tools for the furnishing of Mount Vernon, including about fifty molding planes of various descriptions, as well as a large number of bench and fitting planes.

of turnery for chairs, decorative spindles, table legs, stretchers, and other forms and devices. These elementary machine tools were either individually pedal-driven, spring-pole lathes or big-wheel lathes powered by a helper. In either case the rotating wood was cut away to the required shape by long-handled chisels of various forms. For shaping the curves and corners of flat surfaces— chair seats, table tops, and the like— the craftsman used a frame saw whose cutting blade was always conveniently visible as he worked the saw.

Chair and table stretchers, like the framework of timber buildings and other wooden elements that needed to be firmly fastened together, were joined by mortise and tenon. The tenon, or tongue, of one piece was slipped into the mor- tise, or hole, of the other and the two were then firmly locked by a hardwood pin that was inserted through both. For appearances' sake the mortise often did not go entirely through to the out-

Until the introduction of furniture pattern books about the middle of the eighteenth century the designs of most pieces were based on traditional forms, with such variations as the individual craftsman or his customer may have thought agreeable or necessary. Even in the case of more sophisticated and elegant examples of the late colonial pe-

side surface of a member—hence the term "blind mortise." Shoulders on two or more sides of the tenon kept this element at a fixed angle with the mortised piece. (The craftsman may have used heated animal glue as well, but if a piece was not properly and securely fitted together in the first place no amount of glue would have made a sound joint of the separate elements.)

The most common eighteenth-century device for securing the fronts to the sides of drawers was the dovetail joint, a detail of construction as old in its origins as ancient Egypt. This form of rigid joint, requiring neither nails nor pegs, was also used at other points in the construction of cabinets, boxes, and tables, although the labor involved in tightly fitting the triangular projections into the slots that were cut to receive them was considerable.

These traditional methods of furniture making, a basic but far from inclusive list of procedures, were all involved in the design and construction of such forms as the butterfly table shown here, one of the most pleasing and typical examples of native craftsmanship.

riod, derived from engraved patterns, most pieces were endowed with an individual character which distinguished them from others made in the same style.

Colonial Glassmaking

In the Middle Ages crafts and guilds were referred to as "mysteries," suggesting that secret skills were involved in their occupations. No craft practiced in colonial America better deserved the term than glassmaking. To transform opaque and inert solid materials into a glowing liquid mass that could then be worked into infinitely varied, transparent, and even lustrous shapes required skills and knowledge that to most people bordered on wizardry. Most early American glassmakers were lured from European factories; they followed formulas and methods that had been handed down with little change from century to century. The operations of the colonial craftsman, in fact, differed little from those familiar to the artisans of Sidon, Alexandria, and other glassmaking centers of the ancient Roman Empire.

The essential ingredients of colonial glass were silica, usually in the form of sand, and such alkalies as potash, carbonate of soda or lime, plus certain accessory materials depending on the type and color of glass desired. Much colonial glass was colored, either fortuitously or by intent. Common bottle and window glass, made of relatively unrefined ingredients, was green in color because of certain metallic oxides present as impurities in the raw materials. Other oxides were used to produce artificial colors. However, a clear glass was also produced by the use of black oxide of manganese, called glass soap.

By substituting an oxide of red lead for soda or lime a softer, more lustrous glass—called "lead" or "flint" glass—was achieved. In its clear state this was also called crystal glass, although the word "crystal" had been used for centuries to denote glass of any composition that approached the clarity and purity of rock crystal. (There are as many recipes for glassmaking as there are for making a cake.) These materials, called the "batch," were "cooked" in

clay crucibles that were constructed for the purpose with the same painstaking care that went into the production of the finest porcelain and that were allowed to age for at least a year before they were put to use. Even so the crucibles lasted only a limited

time—a matter of months. Before the glassmaking actually began, the crucibles, or melting pots, were fired to white heat in the furnace; only then were they ready for the batch, to which bits of cleansed and broken glass, called "cullet," had been added to help the fusion of the various ingredients. Under a heat of about 2500 degrees F. these were reduced in a day or two to a molten state. When vitrification was complete the furnace temperature was somewhat lowered to cool the fluid mass to a plastic state in which it could be manipulated.

From that point three basic tools were used to fashion the end product, a blowpipe, a pontil or punty rod, and some sort of shaping tool, although others were used for various special purposes and other factory equipment was required to facilitate the use of those tools. To start, a workman secured from the melting pot a gather of the red-hot glass on a blowpipe and rolled this on the polished surface of a marver to give the material its first shape and an even surface. This blob was then inflated by blowing on the pipe until it reached a workable size and form. The pipe was then handed to the master craftsman, or "gaffer," who sat at a specially designed chair. Resting the pipe on the slanting arms of his chair, the gaffer rolled the pipe with his left hand to keep the blob of glass in constant rotation to prevent it from becoming lopsided. Meanwhile, he manipulated it with his right hand to shape the piece, using a pair of iron tongs (pucellas), and a wooden paddle (battledore) to flatten the bottom. From time to time

as the glass cooled it had to be reheated in the furnace before work could continue; to know just when to do this called for experienced judgment. In the hands of a skilled gaffer the glass could be worked into any conceivable shape. While the glass was still hot other elements could be added to the body of a

piece, such as the stems and bases of glasses, the handles of pitchers, and thin threads or heavier overlays for decorative effects.

To complete the blowpipe end of a form, the punty was fixed to the opposite, or base end by means of a small glob of molten glass; the blowpipe was then detached by touching the wet ends of the pucellas to the hot glass, causing a fracture, and tapping the pipe free. With shears and shaping tools the open end was worked to its final size and outline, such as the rim of a drinking vessel or the curved lip of a pitcher. When the punty was ultimately knocked off the finished piece, it left the rough punty mark on the base, a characteristic of old glass made by such methods.

There were other ways of varying the shape and pattern of glass objects. In the case of many examples that are attributed to Stiegel, for instance, the first gathering of molten glass from the furnace was inflated directly into a small, open-top mold, about one third, or less, the size of the finished article and with intaglio patterns cut into the interior surface of the mold. When the decorative pattern had been impressed on the sufficiently inflated gather, the latter was contracted enough to be withdrawn from the mold and then blown and otherwise fashioned to its final size and shape. As the piece was blown larger the impressed pattern expanded, much like the printed design on a child's balloon, more here, less there, in subtle gradations according to the degree of expansion of the form.

Much of the window glass used in colonial America was of "crown" glass,

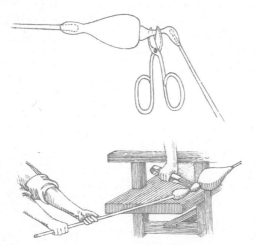

made by blowing a large gathering into a bulbous mass, attaching the punty to the opposite end, and breaking off the blowpipe. The opened "bubble" was then spun vigorously, constantly reheated to keep it workable, until by centrifugal force it reached the form of a relatively flat disc. After it was cooled

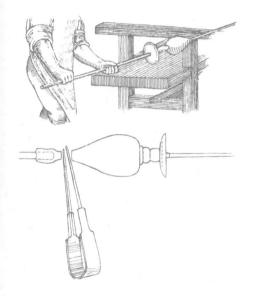

oven. Glass that is cooled too quickly will break into fragments. From beginning to end the process of completing a piece of glass required time for preparation, more time for finishing, and in between quick judgments, co-operative skills, and business organization greater than that of any of the other crafts.

the disc was cut into diamond- or square-shaped panes of glass. The center of the disc, when the punty was knocked off, was an irregularly conical protuberance called a "bull's-eye."

No piece of glass was ready for service until it had been first reheated and then very gradually cooled in an annealing

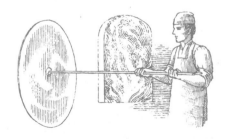

Glossary
of
Terms

Acanthus

Acorn clock

ACANTHUS A stylized decorative motif adapted from the Mediterranean herb; the basis of foliage ornament in classic Greek and Roman designs. The acanthus is particularly evident in Chippendale, Federal, and Empire patterns. See the capital of the column under CLASSICAL ORDER

ACORN A turned decorative motif resembling an acorn. It was often used, for example, as finials on uprights of early colonial chair backs, as pendant ornaments on William and Mary tables, and as ornamentation on Victorian Renaissance Revival forms.

ACORN CLOCK A mid-eighteenth-century Connecticut shelf clock, so-called because its shape suggests an acorn

ADAM BROTHERS Robert (1728–92) and James (1730–94), Scottish architects and designers, who drew from Greek and Roman sources to create a light, graceful style in which interiors, exteriors, and furnishings were harmoniously combined; innovators of the neoclassic patterns so widely interpreted in the Sheraton and Hepplewhite furniture styles

AGATA A type of art glass with mottled decoration formed from mineral or metallic stains, patented in 1887 by the New England Glass Company

AGATEWARE Earthenware pottery originally imported from England in the eighteenth century; so-called because of its resemblance to agate, achieved by mixing varicolored clays

AMBERINA A type of art glass, patented in 1883, which is typically shaded in colors ranging from yellowish-amber to ruby; New England Glass Company

AMBROTYPE A positive photograph on glass, introduced about 1851, made by the collodion process which supplanted the earlier daguerreotype process

AMELUNG, JOHN FREDERICK One of three important glassmakers, all of whom were German-born, working in America in the 1700's. Amelung's glass factory near Frederick, Maryland, was in operation from 1785 to 1795 and was staffed with European-trained craftsmen. Amelung's glass, now museum pieces, was distinguished for its high quality and its fine copper wheel engraving. See also STIEGEL, HENRY WILLIAM, and WISTAR, CASPAR

AMERICAN ORGAN
See CABINET ORGAN

ANGLO-JAPANESE STYLE A style of decoration, developed in England during the 1860's and adapted in America, in which elements of Gothic and Japanese design, freely treated, were incorporated in lightly framed furniture forms and ornamental schemes. The style in America was strongly influenced by the Japanese exhibits at the Philadelphia Centennial International Exhibition of 1876.

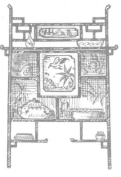

Anglo-Japanese stand

ANIMAL-COVERED DISHES Pressed-glass dishes with covers made in animal forms, generally of the domestic or barnyard variety, such as the widely popular "nesting hen." Animal dishes were produced in great number during the 1880's, chiefly in opaque white or blue glass, combinations of white and blue, or in clear glass.

"Nesting hen"

ANNEALING In silvermaking, the reheating of the metal to keep it malleable while it is being shaped; in glass-

Anthemion

making, the gradual cooling of hot glass to render it less brittle

ANTHEMION A conventional design of flower and leaf forms derived from ancient Greek art, used as an ornamental motif in Greek Revival architecture and on Empire furniture, silver, and glass, as well as Louis XV and XVI Revival styles of the Victorian period; also called Greek honeysuckle pattern

ANTIMACASSAR A name, derived from Macassar hair oil, for the doily used in the Victorian period to protect the back or arms of upholstered furniture; also called a tidy

ANTIMONY An element used in metal alloys, such as pewter and britannia ware, to add strength and a silvery sheen to the finished product

APPLIED ORNAMENT An appliqué; any decorative detail, carved or shaped separately, and then applied, whether on furniture, silver, glass, or needlework

APRON The horizontal piece of wood below a table top, chair seat, looking glass, or underframing of a case piece; frequently carved, pierced, or scalloped; also called a skirt

ARABESQUE A painted, inlaid, or carved design in interlacing patterns of floral, geometric, or figural forms

ARCADING In cabinetwork, the ornamental use of arches in paneling or in openwork

ARCHED STRETCHER An upward-curved or hooped stretcher introduced in the William and Mary period

ARGAND LAMP The first scientifically constructed oil lamp invented in 1783

Argand lamp

by Aimé Argand, a Swiss chemist. A tubular wick was sheltered by a glass chimney, which created a bright light because air currents were contained around the circular flame, thereby increasing combustion. Variations on the controlled-draft principle were applied to numerous new lamp forms, including the kerosene burning lamps that were introduced in 1859. See also ASTRAL LAMP and CARCEL LAMP

ARGUS A 19th-century pressed-glass pattern made of regularly spaced indentations resembling thumbprints

ARMOIRE A tall cupboard or wardrobe, with one or two doors, used for storage of linens and garments; the word, adopted from the French, originally meant a storage cupboard for arms and armor

ARROW-BACK
See WINDSOR CHAIRS

ART GLASS A general term applied to decorative glassware, often of vivid colors and extravagant form, widely produced in America between 1880 and 1910

ART NOUVEAU An international style of design, variously interpreted in different countries in the decades just before and after 1900. The principal motifs were twisted and entwined vines, tendrils, plant forms, and symbolistic female faces or figures with floating, swirling strands of hair. In America Art Nouveau found its chief expression in silver, jewelry, poster art, pottery, metalwork, and glass—such as the glassware designs of Louis Comfort Tiffany.

ARTS AND CRAFTS MOVEMENT The activities undertaken by various groups

Art Nouveau silver brush and Tiffany dragonfly lamp

in the late 19th century in England, and to some extent in America, to improve the quality of industrial art and design, largely through a return to the principles and methods of hand craftsmanship. William Morris was the major prophet of the movement. In this country, the Craftman Workshops near Syracuse, the Rookwood Pottery in Cincinnati, and the Roycrofters in East Aurora, New York, were manifestations of the movement.

ASSAY The test made to determine the quality of metals, such as silver and gold

ASTRAGAL A small, semicircular, convex molding resembling a string of beads. See MOLDINGS for illustration

ASTRAL LAMP A type of Argand lamp, widely used in the 1830's and 1840's, made so that the flattened, ringed cistern holding the oil does not throw a shadow; also called *sinumbra* lamp

AURENE A type of iridescent art glass with a golden sheen in shades of yellow, violet, and pink; introduced late in the 19th century by Steuben Glass Works

Astral lamp

B **ACK STOOL** An early term for a low-back chair without arms; generally upholstered with spool- or spiral-turned legs, stretchers, and back supports. See also CROMWELLIAN FURNITURE

BAG TABLE
See WORK TABLE

BAIL A curving drawer pull, usually brass, hanging from bolts and backed by a decorative plate. See HARDWARE for illustration

BALL-AND-RING An early turning composed of alternating balls and narrow indentations (rings). See TURN-INGS for illustration

BALL FOOT   A round, turned foot used chiefly on furniture of the 17th and early 18th centuries

BALLOON-BACK   A hooped or rounded style of chair back with a pronounced "waistline," particularly associated with Rococo Revival patterns of the Victorian era

BALLROOM CHAIR   A small, delicate, gilt side chair of the Victorian period, usually made with bamboo turnings; easily transported and often rented in large quantities for such festivities as a ball or wedding reception

BALUSTER   An upright support, usually turned and vase shaped, topped by a rail; also called a banister. See TURN-INGS for illustration

BAMBOO FURNITURE   First popularized in the western world in the 18th century through imports from the Orient. In the 1880's and 1890's bamboo furniture was again in vogue, real and simulated, domestic and imported, in western and in oriental designs. Bird's-eye maple, turned in imitation of natural bamboo, was widely used in American manufacture.

BAMBOO TURNINGS   A turning made in a stylized bamboo pattern, sometimes found in Chinese Chippendale designs and introduced about 1790 as a type of leg on American Windsor chairs and on fancy chairs

BANDBOX   A portable box, usually circular, made of pasteboard or thin strips of wood, for the storage or transportation of hats and other small bits of finery; in mid 1800's a popular item,

Ball foot

Balloon-back chair

Simulated bamboo table

Banister-back chair

Banjo clock

decorated with brightly colored printed papers

BANDING　A narrow edging or border of veneer; a contrasting band of inlay. See also STRINGING

BANISTER-BACK CHAIR　A chair with its back made of vertically placed split balusters, usually with the flat sides of the balusters facing front, the rounded sides to the rear; a William and Mary pattern of the 18th century

BANJO CLOCK　A popular term given to the banjo-shaped clock invented by Simon Willard and patented in 1802. The circular dial, elongated shaft, and rectangular base proved so popular a design, that the banjo clock has been continuously and variously reproduced.

BANKS　Toy banks—in glass, tin, wood, or cast iron—extensively manufactured after the Civil War. Mechanical banks, a particular favorite, were made with automaton figures, animated by the deposit of a coin.

BAROQUE　An extravagant style of art and architecture developed in the late 16th and 17th centuries in Europe; characterized by fanciful contortions of classic forms, lavish ornamentation, elaborate scrolls and carvings, twisted columns, and massive oversized forms. The baroque was superseded by the more delicate, asymmetric rococo patterns. In American furniture the baroque style was reflected in William and Mary patterns and in the large-scaled, ornately decorated Louis XIV Revival forms of the mid-Victorian period. The word "baroque," meaning curious or bizarre in French, is derived from the Portuguese *barroco*, an irregularly shaped pearl.

BASKET STAND   A work or sewing stand with two basketlike, spindled tiers mounted on a central column; popularized in the mid 1800's

BAT'S-WING   Popular name for a brass mount, either as a keyhole escutcheon or as the backing of a drawer handle, in the shape of a bat with outspread wings; about 1720–50. See HARDWARE

BAUHAUS   A revolutionary school of art and architecture, founded by Walter Gropius in Germany in 1919, that approached problems of design by considering all the arts and crafts in terms of modern materials and industrial methods.

BEAD-AND-REEL   A round molding or turning of alternating oval beads with disks. See MOLDINGS for illustration

BEADING   A fine-scale, beadlike, semicircular molding

BEADWORK   A type of Victorian needlework, the beads strung and then stitched into flowery designs on such items as watchcases, cushions, wall pockets, and penwipers

BEAKER   The early name for a large drinking cup with a wide mouth

BED WARMER
See WARMING PAN

BEEHIVE CLOCK   A type of small Connecticut shelf clock with the wooden case rounding to a point at the top, made in the mid 1800's; so-called because of its resemblance to an old-fashioned beehive; sometimes known as a flatiron clock, because the pointed case resembled the rounded point of an iron. See also LANCET CLOCK

BELLEEK   A fragile, featherweight, translucent, porcelainlike ware with a

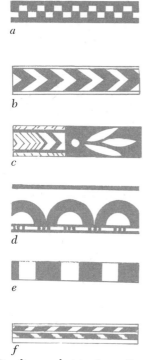

a

b

c

d

e

f

Banding and stringing patterns of the Federal period characteristic of: (a) Massachusetts. (b) New Hampshire. (c) Massachusetts. (d) Massachusetts. (e) Connecticut. (f) Maryland

Bellflower

pearly glaze; first manufactured by David McBirney & Company, Belleek, Ireland; produced in America from about 1882

BELLFLOWER   Floral ornament with a bud of three or five pointed, narrow petals; popular as an inlay pattern on Federal furniture, and also on pressed glass of the early Victorian period

BELL JAR   Bell-shaped glass dome, particularly associated with Victorian *décor*; bell jars served to protect such ornamental displays as stuffed birds, bouquets of waxed flowers, or other dust-catching fancies

BELTER, JOHN HENRY   (1804–63) German-American cabinetmaker who worked in New York City, roughly from 1840 to 1860; famed for his curvilinear Rococo Revival furniture of the early Victorian period. Using the stylish woods of the era, such as rosewood and mahogany, and his patented laminating process, Belter produced sinuously shaped forms that were lavishly carved and pierced with intricate designs.

BENNINGTON WARE   An earthenware with a mottled or streaked brown glaze properly called Rockingham ware, from the estate of the Marquis of Rockingham, Yorkshire, England, where this type of glaze was first produced in the 18th century. The ware is popularly known as Bennington in America because of its extensive manufacture at the Bennington, Vermont potteries, although it was also made in countless factories throughout the country from about 1835 to the close of the century in innumerable patterns — from pie plates, bowls, teapots, and pitchers to door knobs, picture frames, spittoons, and animal figurines.

Belter chair

BENTWOOD FURNITURE   Furniture made from wood that has been bent and shaped, as were the bowed backs of Windsor chairs. Bentwood is now popularly associated with the extravagantly curved chairs and tables, molded by steam and pressure, that were first developed in Germany by Michael Thonet in the 1830's and manufactured in Austria in the 1840's. Imports to America were soon copied and have been continuously made in various forms.

Bentwood chair

BERGÈRE   A French term for an upholstered and commodious chair, with closed arms and usually with a loose seat cushion; commonly designed in the Louis XV style

BERLIN WORK   Wool needle-point embroidery, popularized in the mid-19th century; so-called from the pre-patterned backgrounds stamped on canvas and the brightly colored wools exported from Berlin. Covers for footstools and pillows, patterns for traveling bags, bedroom slippers, gentlemen's suspenders and vests were but a few of the Berlin work designs available.

BETTY LAMP   A lighting device of ancient origin, used into the 19th century in rural areas and on the frontier; usually iron or tin with a shallow reservoir for grease and the floating wick; designed either as a standing lamp or as a hanging lamp. Among the many suggested derivations of the name, Betty lamp may be an abbreviation of "better lamp," the term used to describe an improved form with a separate wick holder. Also known as judies, kays, frog lamps, and phoebes

BEZEL   A grooved rim; in clockmak-

Betty lamp

ing the rim into which a clockface glass is secured

BIBELOT   A small decorative object or one of novel interest; from an early French word meaning a bauble or plaything

BIBLE BOX   An early colonial, carved wooden box to hold books or writing materials; made with a hinged, often sloping, lid

Bible box

BIEDERMEIER   A German furniture style, popular from about 1825 to 1860, that was largely derived from French Empire forms and characterized by a rather heavy-handed interpretation of classic forms. The name supposedly comes from Papa Biedermeier, a German newspaper's comic caricature of substantial, middle-class well-being.

BIRD CAGE   A device with four short balusters and central pivot, fitted between the top and the shaft of a tripod table, designed to allow the top to be rotated and tilted; used on American tilt-top tables during latter half of the 1700's; sometimes called a squirrel cage

BISCUIT WARE   Unglazed pottery or porcelain; popularly called bisque, an abbreviation of the French *biscuit*, or twice-baked; first developed at the Sèvres porcelain works in France about 1750. In the latter part of the 1800's biscuit ware figurines and bric-a-brac of all varieties were extensively exported from France and Germany to America.

BISQUE
See BISCUIT WARE

BLACK GLASS   A general term given to bottle glass which can range in color from dark green to dark purple

BLANKET CHEST A chest on short legs, for the storage of blankets and linens, often with one or two drawers below; introduced in the mid 1600's

BLANKET RAIL The rail or stretcher between the two supporting posts at the foot of a bed

BLOCK FOOT An enlarged square block of wood terminating a plain, straight leg. See MARLBOROUGH LEG for illustration

BLOCK-FRONT The front of a case piece, such as a desk or chest of drawers, cut in such a fashion that the center section recedes and the two outer sections curve forward. Apparently a purely American design of the Chippendale period and associated with the cabinetwork of Newport, Rhode Island. In Newport patterns a carved shell generally topped each of the three block-front sections. The style, at the time, was known as "swelled front." See also GODDARD and TOWNSEND

Block-front Chippendale desk

BLOWN-MOLDED GLASS Glass blown into a small mold to impress a pattern or establish a shape, then withdrawn and expanded into final form by further blowing and manipulation; one of the most ancient of glass-blowing techniques

BLOWN THREE-MOLD GLASS Glass impressed with a design from a full-size, three-part, hinged mold. Believed to have been an American development, the technique was devised to imitate the patterns of cut glass and was popular from about 1815 to 1830, when it was superseded by the invention of mechanical glass pressing.

BOBÊCHE A plain or ornamental disk, often of glass, set on the candle

Blown three-mold pitcher

Bohemian ruby compote

Bombé Chippendale secretary

*Bonnet-top Queen Anne
secretary*

socket of a candlestick, chandelier, or sconce to catch the drippings

BOHEMIAN GLASS A trade name for mid-19th-century glass with one or more layers of colored glass cut away in patterns revealing the clear glass body. The name was derived from a German glass, particularly suitable for engraving and overlay, that was extensively exported from Bohemia early in the 1800's. Also called cased or overlay glass

BOMBÉ A term applied to furniture with rounded or bulging front and sides, the word adopted from the French adjective meaning swollen or bulging; a baroque form used in Chippendale designs. Also called a kettle base

BONE CHINA An artificial porcelain, hard and translucent, made with white bone ash instead of kaolin, the natural china clay; first developed in England in the mid 1700's

BONE DISH A crescent-shaped side dish used in Victorian table settings for such discards as bones or fruit pits

BONHEUR-DU-JOUR A small ladies' desk developed in France during the 18th century, the rectangular, flat-front desk cabinet set back upon its supporting frame; made with a pull-out writing board or a fall-front writing board; frequently surmounted with marble and a fretwork metal gallery

BONNET TOP A broken, scrolled pediment forming a hood from front to back atop tall case furniture of the Chippendale period, favored in Rhode Island design

BOSS An oval or circular applied ornament, usually ebonized; typically applied to chests and cupboards of 17th-century colonial design

BOSTON CHAIR   Type of 18th-century, high-back chair, so-named because of extensive manufacture in and around Boston; seats and backs were either caned or covered in leather; usually made of maple, and often painted red or black

Boston chair

BOSTON ROCKER   A rocking chair, developed from the Windsor chair and introduced in America about 1835, with a wooden seat curving down at the front and up at the back. The high back was made of vertical spindles beneath a wide crest rail, usually painted or stenciled with ornamental detail. See also **SALEM ROCKER**

BOTTLE GLASS
See **GREEN GLASS**

BOTTLE TICKET   A small plaque, often of silver, hung by a chain around the neck of a decanter, the plaque labeled with the name of the beverage in the decanter

BOUILLOTTE CANDELABRUM   A table lamp with dish-shaped base supporting a shaft fitted with two or three candle brackets and a metal shade surmounted by a finial. The name comes from the French card game of *bouillotte*.

BOULLE   An elaborate form of marquetry created with such materials as tortoise shell, brass, silver, pewter, or ivory; invented by the French cabinetmaker André-Charles Boulle under the patronage of Louis XIV

BOW-BACK
See **WINDSOR CHAIRS**

BOW-FRONT   Term for the rounded,

Bouillotte candelabrum

outward-curving front of Chippendale case pieces — chests of drawers, sideboards, and so forth

BRACE-BACK
See WINDSOR CHAIRS

BRACKET A shaped, often pierced decorative support bracing the leg to a chair seat, table top, or body of a case piece; also, a small decorative shelf, or simply the brace upon which the shelf rests

Fretwork brackets on Chippendale table

BRACKET CLOCK A type of small clock popularized with the introduction of the short pendulum in 1658; often set in a domed case fitted with a handle; produced in varying contemporary patterns until the early 1800's; principally an English import, the name presumably derived from the matching brackets of late 18th- and early 19th-century models

BRACKET FOOT A foot shaped like a bracket with mitered corners, often scrolled on the free sides, and found on case furniture; particularly popular on Chippendale and Federal furniture

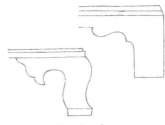

Bracket feet

BRASS BEDSTEAD A type of metal bedstead, generally ornamented with many knobs and finials; produced in America in enormous quantities toward the close of the 19th century and into the first decade of the 20th century; equally as popular as the cast-iron bedsteads of the period

BRAZIER
See CHAFING DISH

BREADBOARD ENDS The ends of a plank table finished with strips of wood that cover the raw edges and also guard against warping

BREAKFRONT A large case piece with

a center section that is projected forward, thus "breaking" the otherwise flat, front surface; usually surmounted by a pediment; a pattern introduced in the 18th century

BREWSTER CHAIR A Pilgrim armchair, heavily turned, with a rush or wooden seat and rows of spindles on the back, below the arms, and below the seat; named after Elder William Brewster of the Plymouth colony. The Carver chair of the same period had spindles only across the back.

BRISTOL Opaque blown glass, first manufactured in England in the late 1700's; in the Victorian period, American manufacture was most typically in opaque white glass with rose or blue lining and crimped or ruffled edges.

BRITANNIA WARE A trade name given to a type of pewter originally developed in England about 1750; the silverlike alloy consisting of tin, antimony, and copper lent itself to mass production; extensively produced in America from about 1830 to 1860

BROKEN PEDIMENT A triangular or curved pediment having a gap at the apex. See PEDIMENT for illustration

BUCKET BENCH
See WATER BENCH

BUHL
See BOULLE

BULL'S-EYE
See CROWN GLASS

BULL'S-EYE MIRROR
See CONVEX MIRROR

BULTOS Statues of holy persons or objects carved from wood, frequently plastered with gesso, and brightly painted; made in Mexico and New

Brewster chair

Bun foot

Butterfly table

Eastlake cabinet organ

Mexico (now New Mexico, Arizona, Colorado, and Texas) from about 1750 in the provincial patterns derived from Mexican baroque art and architecture. See also SANTOS and RETABLOS

BUN FOOT A slightly flattened, round foot extending from a small turned shaft, used chiefly on furniture of 17th and early 18th centuries

BUREAU A chest of drawers, the term having come into popular usage in America early in the 1800's. In England a bureau is a desk, as it is in the original French meaning.

BURL A protruding, irregularly grained growth on a tree; used in sections as a thin veneer, or hollowed into bowls

BURMESE A type of opaque art glass resembling porcelain in its shaded color and glossy surface; first produced in America in 1885 by the Mount Washington Glass Company, New Bedford, Massachusetts

BUTTERFLY HINGE A butterfly-shaped hinge with the pivot at the narrow part; also called dovetail hinge

BUTTERFLY TABLE A drop-leaf table with solid brackets, resembling wings or rudders, to support the leaves; an American colonial pattern of the 1700's

BUTTERFLY WEDGE A butterfly-shaped wedge of wood or metal used to join two pieces of wood or stone

CABINETMAKER A general term for a skilled worker in wood; one who makes fine furniture or the interior woodwork of houses

CABINET ORGAN A musical instrument, also known as the American organ and very popular in the late 19th century, the tones produced by the vibration of differently shaped and sized reeds

CABOCHON A round or oval ornamentation with a smooth surface, named for the rounded, unfaceted cutting of a precious stone. The cabochon motif was popular, for example, as decoration on the knees of cabriole legs of the Chippendale period.

CABRIOLE A reverse-curved leg ending in a shaped foot that was extremely popular during the Queen Anne and Chippendale periods and in the 19th-century revival of past styles

CACHEPOT A decorative container for a flowerpot; a French term meaning "pot hider"

CADDY A small box, can, or chest originally intended for the storage of tea; the name derived from *kati*, a Malay weight of slightly over a pound

CAMPAIGN FURNITURE Portable and often folding furniture, originally designed for the military and adapted for household use. For example: folding, cotlike camp beds were recommended early in the mid 1800's for use in cottages and country homes; folding, canvas-seated camp stools were popularized at the same time; the wooden-framed, collapsible officer's chair (now commonly known as a director's chair) was made in the Victorian period with the seat and back either of canvas, needlepoint, or carpeting. See also **FIELD BED**

CAMPHENE LAMP About 1830 to 1860; typically in pewter, britannia ware, or tin, a font with a shaped standard. Camphene, used in the same sort of

Cabriole leg

Tilt-top candlestand

lamps as whale oil, was a mixture of turpentine and alcohol, highly inflammable. The wicks, therefore, were taller than whale-oil wicks and slanted well apart. Camphene lamps usually have metal snuffers or caps attached by a small chain.

CANDELABRUM A candleholder with several arms or branches, popularly used in the plural, candelabra

CANDLEBOX A wooden or tin box for the storage of candles, sometimes designed to hang on the wall

CANDLESTAND A small stand or table, usually a tripod, suitable for holding a candlestick or lamp, as well as various small decorative objects; introduced early in the 1700's. Provincial forms included a screw type candlestand, the adjustable candle arm on a threaded pole.

CANE Split rattan used to weave chair backs and seats; introduced to Europe in the 16th century by way of the East India trade; first used in America as a fashionable feature of William and Mary chairs and day beds

CANNON-BALL BED Popular term for a type of bed, about 1820–50, with four turned posts, each topped with a ball finial, hence the nickname "cannon-ball bed"; typically made with a shaped headboard, rarely with a matching footboard, but with a blanket rail at the end of the bed; a pattern particularly favored by country cabinetmakers

CANOPY
See TESTER

CANTERBURY A low stand, usually on casters, made of vertical openwork partitions, for holding music and papers; so-named, according to Sheraton's *Cabinet Dictionary* (1803), because the first such piece had been ordered by an Archbishop of Canterbury

CANTON WARE   The popular name given to a blue and white Chinese ware exported in enormous quantities to America from the opening days of the China trade in the 1780's; manufactured in China until the 1950's

CAPE COD LIGHTER   A jug-shaped metal container in which a lighter soaks in kerosene. The lighter is made of a porous material, such as baked clay, affixed to a metal handle and when placed under firewood holds a flame until the wood catches.

CAPTAIN'S CHAIR
See WINDSOR CHAIRS

CAPTAIN'S CHEST   A chest of drawers with flat recessed brass drawer pulls, that divides into two portable sections readily carried by the brass handles affixed on each side; an 18th-century design both for the field and for shipboard; also known as a campaign chest and reproduced to this day

CAPTAIN'S DECANTER   A glass decanter with a broad flat base to prevent tipping when the ship rolled in a heavy sea; 18th and 19th centuries

CARCEL LAMP   A variation of the Argand lamp, with a clockwork pump to keep the burner filled with oil from the reservoir below; a French invention of 1800, used until about 1850; also called a mechanized lamp

CARD TABLE   A furniture form appearing late in the 17th century, prompted by the craze for card games and gambling; usually made with a folding top, the playing surface covered with green baize; early examples often have depression at the corners to hold candle-

Queen Anne card table

sticks and scooped-out holes for money or chips. Also known as a gaming table

CARNIVAL GLASS Pressed iridescent glass in imitation of finer iridescent glassware, so-named because it was a giveaway at fairs and carnivals in the early 1900's; also called taffeta glass or poor man's Tiffany

CARPETBAG A portable traveling bag popular in the latter half of the 19th century, often stitched in brightly colored needle-point patterns; so-called because such bags were originally made of carpeting

CARRIAGE CLOCK The name popularly given to clocks enclosed in a square glass case, mounted in brass, with a handle on the top. A late Victorian fashion, introduced from France, derived from earlier, portable clocks designed for travel; hence the name "carriage clock"

CARTOUCHE A decorative motif in the form of a shield or partially unrolled scroll with curled edges

Cartouche

CARVER CHAIR A Pilgrim chair, usually with a rush seat, similar in turnings to the Brewster chair, but with spindles only on the back; named for a chair belonging to Governor John Carver of the Plymouth colony and supposedly brought on the *Mayflower*

CARYATID A supporting column in the form of a female figure developed in ancient Greece and since used in architecture and furniture, principally an Empire motif

CASED GLASS
See **BOHEMIAN GLASS**

CASE FURNITURE A general term for boxlike furniture, such as secretaries,

Carver chair

bookcases, cabinets, chests of drawers, and so forth

CASTELLATED Pierced in a regular pattern, as on the parapets of fortified structures; used also on some Gothic and Gothic Revival furniture as an ornamental device

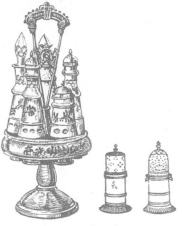

CASTER A shaker for sugar or pepper or dry mustard, sometimes known as a dredger; also, a stand with cruets and containers for condiments; also, a small roller or wheel set into the feet or the base of furniture to facilitate moving

Cruet stand and casters

CAST-IRON FURNITURE Very popular throughout the 19th century in varying forms from garden furniture and plant stands, to umbrella racks and doorstops. One of the most ubiquitous forms of all, the cast-iron bedstead, was widely manufactured in the late Victorian period and into the early years of the 20th century.

CAUDLE CUP A two-handled cup, often with a cover, used to serve a warm drink of spice-sweetened wine or ale; a silver form introduced in the 1600's and popular in America until the 1720's

Cast-iron garden bench

CAULIFLOWER WARE Descriptive name of a type of pottery with green leaves and white flower clusters in imitation of a cauliflower; first produced in England in the 18th century

CAVETTO A concave molding, usually one-quarter round in section. See MOLDINGS for illustration

CELLARET A cabinet for wine, liquors, glasses, and so forth; also a deep drawer for bottles in a sideboard

CHAFING DISH The American term

Chair-table

for a brazier; a footed, long-handled vessel designed to hold burning charcoal over which plates of food were kept warm; introduced in America in the 17th century; now largely a device for cooking food at the table

CHAIR-TABLE Chair with a hinged top that folds down to form a table; introduced in the 17th century; also known by the modern term, monk's chair. See also HUTCH TABLE

CHAISE LONGUE The French term for a long chair or day bed, introduced as a fashionable piece of furniture in France in the 18th century

CHALKWARE Unglazed, molded plaster of Paris figurines, colored with oil paints or with water colors, originating in Europe. The provincial forms, in naïve imitation of porcelain ornaments, were once attributed to the Pennsylvania Germans, but the first-known domestic manufacture was in Boston in the late 1700's. Throughout the 1800's chalkware was widely made by Italian immigrant "folk artists."

CHAMBERSTICK A small candlestick with a saucerlike base and handle, designed to light the way to one's chamber at bedtime. Early types were often of the so-called "frying-pan" pattern, a flat base with a broad, flat handle. From 1750 to the early 1800's, chambersticks typically were made with a shaped base, ring handle, and a cone-shaped snuffer in a slot at the side of the socket; made in silver, brass, pewter, Sheffield plate, and pottery.

CHAMFER In woodworking, the flat surface made by smoothing off or planing an angle or an edge

CHASING A decoration on metal surfaces produced by a relatively blunt instrument that indents but does not cut into the surface

CHEST OF DRAWERS A furniture form that came into general use in the 17th century, superseding the chest as a storage space. See also BUREAU

William and Mary chest of drawers

CHEST-ON-CHEST The term for a double chest of drawers, introduced in England about 1700, widely used in America after 1750; also known as a tallboy, as opposed to the highboy which is set on legs

CHEST-ON-FRAME A 17th-century design that lifted the storage chest and drawers off the floor to a convenient height; a forerunner of the full chest of drawers

CHEVAL GLASS A full-length mirror mounted on a tilting or swinging mechanism between two upright supporting columns; introduced in the last quarter of the 18th century, when production of plate glass was so perfected that full-length mirrors could be manufactured. The name is derived from the French *cheval*, or horse, meaning a supporting framework, as it does in such English terms as "sawhorse."

Chippendale chest-on-chest

CHEVRON A V-shaped decorative motif found, for example, in inlay work of the Federal period

CHIFFONIER A tall, narrow chest of drawers, often surmounted with an attached mirror in the late Victorian period when the term became popular in America; originally, in French cabinetwork, a tall chest of drawers in which ladies kept odds and ends of needlework and fabric swatches; from the French word *chiffon*, flimsy bits of cloth

CHIMNEY GLASS
See OVERMANTEL MIRROR

Chest-on-frame

CHINA CLAY
See PORCELAIN

CHINA STONE
See PORCELAIN

CHINA PAINTING While the hand painting of china is an ancient professional art, it became a craze among ladies of the Victorian era and reached its height after the Centennial Exhibition, with any number of so-called amateur china painters demonstrating skill and accomplishment in their craft. At the height of the china painting vogue, the demand for undecorated forms—or blanks—was so great that they were not only domestically produced but widely imported, often in fine French porcelains.

CHINESE EXPORT PORCELAIN The ceramic ware made and decorated in China for export to the Occident from the early 16th to the mid-19th centuries; often misleadingly termed Lowestoft

Chinese export teapot

CHINESE CHIPPENDALE An adaptation of Chinese motifs into furniture designs of the 18th century, popularized through Thomas Chippendale's versions of the contemporary vogue

CHINOISERIE Chinese art and decoration adapted into Western designs; introduced in the 17th century through Europe's expanding trade with the Far East

CHIP CARVING Simple carving in soft wood, the patterns in low relief

CHIPPENDALE, THOMAS (1718–79) English cabinetmaker and designer whose pattern manual, *The Gentleman and Cabinet-maker's Director*, first published in 1754, influenced styles both in England and America; hence the label "Chippendale" for furniture of that period, in which his masterful designs were so widely copied.

CHIPPENDALE STYLE (1750 to 1785) In essence a rococo style, the bold Chippendale forms embellished with such graceful motifs as Chinese fretwork, Gothic traceries, and French shellwork, foliage, gadrooning, and scrolls. Classic revival pediments were used atop case pieces, with the highboy reaching the peak of its development, cabriole and Marlborough legs were featured; mahogany was the favorite wood, and elaborately carved, pierced chair backs were an innovation over earlier splat-back chairs of the Queen Anne style.

CHROMOLITHOGRAPH A colored picture printed from a series of lithographic stones or plates, one for each of several colors; particularly suited for inexpensive color reproductions of oil paintings; enormously popular in the Victorian era. See also PRANG, LOUIS

CIGAR-STORE INDIANS Life-sized, carved wooden Indians, typically used as eye-catching advertisements in front of American tobacconists' shops throughout the country from about 1850 to the early 1900's. The brightly painted Indian maidens and Indian chiefs, frequently carved with one arm extended to display wooden cigars, were a uniquely American development in the old tradition of shop figures — a horse's head over a livery stable, an oriental figure in front of a tea shop. Tobacconists also advertised with full-sized figures representing such varied characters as a Scottish Highlander, a Turk, Mr. Pickwick, or Sir Walter Raleigh.

Chippendale highboy, chair, and stool

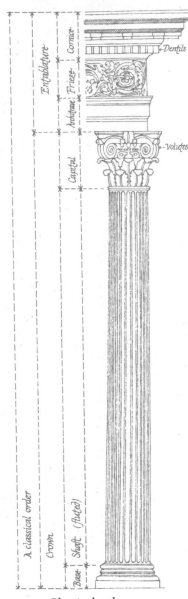

Classical order

CIPHER   Interweaving of initials in a monogram, often surrounded by a decorative scroll

CLASSICAL ORDER   The formal arrangement of columns or pilasters, including their base moldings and capitals and their entablatures, as developed in ancient Greece and Rome and revived during the Renaissance. The elements and proportions represented in the classical order were widely copied and adapted in architecture and furniture in 18th-century England, thence into American design.

CLAW-AND-BALL   A carved foot resembling a bird's claw holding a ball, commonly used as the termination of a cabriole leg in the Chippendale period; adapted from an ancient oriental design of a dragon's claw holding a pearl

CLOSESTOOL
See COMMODE

COCK'S-HEAD HINGE   A type of hinge whose terminations are shaped in the form of a cock's head; a design of medieval origin used in colonial America

COIN SILVER   Although silver coins were often melted down for use by early colonial silversmiths, the term coin silver refers to those pieces stamped coin, pure coin, or dollar, or with the initials C or D. These marks were occasionally put on silver, roughly between 1830 and 1860, to indicate that the silver content was equal to that of United States coin — 900 parts of pure silver out of 1000. See also STERLING

COLONIAL   The period before the American Revolution, the furniture styles being: Jacobean (or Pilgrim), William and Mary, Queen Anne, and Chippendale. The term colonial is frequently and mistakenly applied to such post-Revolutionary furniture as the Federal and Empire styles.

COLONIAL REVIVAL STYLE A style in late 19th-century architecture, furniture, and decoration that imitated or freely adapted designs of colonial and subsequent early American periods

COLT REVOLVERS As patented by Samuel Colt in 1836, the first practical repeating gun in American firearms, the cylinder revolving automatically when the hammer was cocked. Various models were produced at Colt's factory in Hartford, Connecticut, including a .36 caliber Navy revolver in 1851 and a .44 caliber revolver widely used in the Civil War. The grips were often carved, and made of bone, special woods, or silver.

Colonial Revival dressing table

COMB-BACK
See WINDSOR CHAIRS

COMET
See HORN OF PLENTY

COMMODE A low chest of drawers or a cabinet on legs, from the French, meaning "convenient." In the Victorian period the term was used for a closed stool or a cupboard designed to hold a chamber pot, such cupboards often combined with a washstand.

CONCH Inlaid or painted ornamentation resembling such a shell, often appearing on Federal style furniture

CONFIDANTE The name sometimes given to the Victorian three-way chair, which consisted of three seats arranged in a circular design. See also CONVERSATIONAL, a related chair design seating two people

Claw-and-ball foot

Cock's-head hinge

Conch

*Connecticut Valley
sunflower chest*

CONNECTICUT VALLEY SUNFLOWER CHEST 17th- and early 18th-century chests, principally made in the Connecticut River valley; decorated with applied split spindles and applied ebonized bosses and carved panels of stylized sunflowers and tulips

CONSOLE TABLE A side table without back legs, the top supported by one or more brackets or consoles; often fixed to the wall beneath a mirror. See also PIER TABLE

CONSTITUTION MIRROR The name popularly given to a rectangular looking glass of Chippendale design, about 1750-75; the gilt architectural frame is topped with a broken-arch pediment, with an ornamental device such as an eagle or an urn; the bottom of the frame is bordered with a shaped apron.

CONVERSATIONAL An S-shaped seat designed so that two people could sit face to face. The pattern is believed to have originated with furnishings designed in the 1850's for the Empress Eugénie of France; also called a tête-à-tête

Victorian conversational

CONVEX MIRROR A circular mirror with a convex glass, the elaborate gilt frame decorated with gilt balls and surmounted by a spread eagle; largely imported from England and France, where the pattern originated, and popular in America throughout the Federal and Empire periods. When candle arms were added, convex mirrors were known as girandole mirrors.

CONVOLUTE A coiled or scrolled form

CORAL GLASS
See PEACHBLOW

CORNER BLOCK Triangular block set

in the corners of chair and other frames as reinforcement

CORNER CHAIR An open-back chair, introduced in the early 1700's, designed to fit in the corner of a room; often used as a desk chair, because it could accommodate full skirts; also known as a roundabout chair

Queen Anne corner chair

CORNER CUPBOARD Cupboard shaped to fit in a corner, often designed in architectural forms as an integral part of the room; particularly associated with 18th-century *décor.*

CORNER TABLE A table shaped to fit into a corner, often made in pairs and frequently decorated during the Federal period with marquetry or lacquer work and fitted with a marble top; also called an encoignure

CORNICE In architecture, the uppermost division of an entablature; also the projecting molding at the top of a window or large case piece. See CLASSICAL ORDER for illustration

Cornucopia

CORNUCOPIA Carved, inlaid, or painted ornamentation resembling a horn of plenty often appearing on furniture of the Federal and Empire styles

COTTAGE FURNITURE A term used in the Victorian period for mass-produced simplified forms, frequently painted with decorative designs; often ornamented with spool turnings

COUNTRY FURNITURE A general term for furniture made by provincial craftsmen; therefore, furniture in relatively simple patterns, using native woods. As a rule, traditional provincial designs were freely mixed with modest adaptations of contemporary furniture styles fashionable in urban centers.

Cottage dresser

Court cupboard

COURT CUPBOARD A rectangular cupboard of the early colonial period, either with an enclosed, recessed cabinet above and an open bottom shelf, or two tiers of open shelves

COURTING MIRROR Term for a small mirror with crudely painted glass insets in the wooden crest and frame, originally fitted into a shallow box with a sliding cover; imported from northern Europe in the late 18th and early 19th centuries

COVE A large, concave molding generally applied to cornices. See MOLDINGS for illustration

COVERLET A bed cover, from the French *couvrir* plus *lit*. The term now popularly refers to the hand-loomed coverlets woven in two- or three-color geometric patterns from homespun and home-dyed yarns, most typically in blue and white, or red, blue, and white, or green and white. Early American coverlets were made from two or three strips of homespun sewn together. With the introduction of the full-length loom about 1830, coverlets were woven in one piece, usually by a professional neighborhood weaver to whom the housewife brought her homemade yarns.

COZY CORNER
See TURKISH CORNER

CRADLE ROCKER
See ROCKING BENCH

CRAFTSMAN FURNITURE Furniture in the Mission style made and marketed by Gustav Stickley from 1901 to his bankruptcy in 1915. See also STICKLEY, GUSTAV and ROYCROFT STUDIOS

CRANBERRY GLASS Popular in the

1880's, generally of simple design; the pink-red color achieved by the addition of oxide of gold to the molten glass

CRANE A swinging iron bracket used to hang cooking utensils in a fireplace

CRAZY QUILT An elaborate, late Victorian version of the traditional patchwork quilt. Crazy quilts were made from irregularly shaped scraps of brocade, velvet, silk, and satin sewn in asymmetric patterns, the seams covered with silk embroidery work such as feather stitching.

CREAMWARE A lead-glazed, ivory-colored earthenware perfected by Josiah Wedgwood in the 1760's; commonly known as "Queen's Ware," in homage to Queen Charlotte. Exports in the early 1800's from such English pottery centers as Liverpool, Newcastle, and Leeds were generally decorated with transfer-printed designs of American patriotic emblems, presidential portraits, naval scenes, and so forth. By 1840 American firms were imitating creamware, but it was never comparable to English imports. See also **LEEDS WARE**

CREST RAIL The top rail of a chair, settee, or any other seating form

CREWELWORK A type of needlework using embroidery of worsted yarn on linen or cotton. Crewelwork patterns adapted from oriental textile motifs — vines, leaves, flowers, birds, insects — were first popularized in England during the 1600's.

Renaissance Revival crest rail

CRICKET A low, wooden foot stool, usually with three splayed legs; typical of colonial design

CRIMPER A tool used for decorating a rim of glass, metal, or other materials with a wavy, undulating line

Crocket

Cromwell chair

CROCKET   A carved, projecting ornament, of curved and bent foliage, used on the sloping edge of spires and gables in Gothic and Gothic Revival architecture; sometimes used to decorate furniture in those styles

CROMWELLIAN FURNITURE   Side chairs, armchairs, and settees introduced in England during Cromwell's regime (1649–60); the severe, square-backed lines reproduced in the American colonies during the latter part of the 1600's, typically with spiral or ball turnings, and leather or turkeywork upholstery

CROSS-STRETCHER   A horizontal brace in the form of an X connecting the legs of chairs, tables, and case pieces

CROWN GLASS   A type of early blown glass, spun rapidly at the end of a punty rod to form a flat disc, from which panes of glass were cut. A scar or knob of glass, called a bull's-eye, remained in the center of the disc, where it had been attached to the punty rod.

CROWN MILANO   A type of art glass, white opal in color, with raised enamel decoration; Mount Washington Glass Company, New Bedford, Massachusetts, 1886–95

CRYSTAL   A term used for clear, brilliant glass of excellent quality commonly containing lead oxide; also called flint or lead glass

C-SCROLL   A scroll carved in the form of the letter C

CULLET   In glassmaking, cleansed and broken glass remelted with each new batch to promote fusion

CUPID'S BOW   A shaped top rail resembling a bow, commonly used on

C-scroll

chairs of the Chippendale period

CUP PLATE A small glass plate to hold a teacup, after the hot tea was poured from the cup into its matching saucer, to be cooled and drunk—a tea-drinking quirk of the first half of the 19th century, that seems to have originated in Europe, as did cup plates. Early examples were imports of porcelain and pottery. American manufacturers of pressed glass quickly dominated the local market with lacy-glass plates, impressed with such patterns as sunbursts, hearts, historical motifs, eagles, ships, and portraits of notables.

CUP TURNING A turning resembling an inverted bowl or cup common on William and Mary furniture. See TURNINGS for illustration

CURRIER AND IVES A lithography firm (1857–1910) founded in New York City by Nathaniel Currier and James Merritt Ives. The inexpensive prints, of over seven thousand different subjects, were continually popular in Victorian *décor*.

CURULE CHAIR Chair with an X-shaped support, known as "Grecian Cross" legs, derived from an ancient form used by Roman dignitaries; variously interpreted in Sheraton, early Empire, and Victorian designs

Curule chair

CUSP A Gothic ornamental detail, consisting of a point or knob frequently carved, projecting from the intersection of two curves

CUSPIDOR A low, round vessel; the word derived from Portuguese, meaning "one who spits." See also SPITTOON

CURTAIN HOLDER
See TIEBACK

Cusp

Cut-glass compote

CUTCARD A flat decoration cut from thin silver sheets and applied to the surface of a piece of silver

CUT GLASS Glass ornamented by grinding and polishing to produce more or less elaborate designs, principally geometric. As a symbol of elegance, cut glass reached its peak of popularity in America following the Philadelphia Centennial Exhibition in 1876, where glassworks and cutting shops were on display, with countless pieces sold and given away as Centennial souvenirs.

CUTWORK A 19th-century decorative art; delicate patterns, flowers, figures, and scenes cut from paper; a fashionable fad among Victorian ladies, with cutwork often silhouetted and framed or used as a lacy trim on valentines and other such pretty mementoes. Also known as *papyrotamia*, the Latin word meaning "paper cutting"

CYMA A double curve; a cyma recta is concave above and convex below, a cyma reversa, convex above and concave below; also called an ogee. See MOLDINGS for illustration

DAGUERREOTYPE A photograph made by a process developed in France by Louis J. Daguerre, in which a silver or silver-covered copper plate is made sensitive to light by the action of chemicals. The process, which was made public in France in 1839, was superseded in the 1850's with the invention of collodion-coated photographic plates.

DAISY-IN-DIAMOND A pattern-molded design particularly associated with American glassware; a daisylike flower enclosed within a four-sided diamond shape; among earliest examples is expanded-mold daisy-in-diamond patterned glass by Stiegel. Daisy-in-hexagon is an elaborate variation. See STIEGEL, WILLIAM HENRY for illustration

DAISY-IN-HEXAGON See DAISY-IN-DIAMOND

DAMASCUS TABLE A small, low, side table, usually inlaid, in the Moorish style; popularized in America in the late Victorian years during the craze for Near Eastern *décor*

Damascus table

DAVENPORT Upholstered sofa, often convertible into a bed, a late 19th-century American term; also a small desk of a type originating in England in the early 1800's, typically with drawers in the side and a slope front, lift lid

DAY BED In America the day bed was first produced in the mid 1600's as an elongated bench, usually caned and covered with loose cushions. The French term *chaise longue*, or long chair, has come into general use for this type of furniture, while the term day bed is now an inclusive word for a variety of dual purpose couches, used both for seating and for sleeping.

Golden oak davenport

DEDHAM WARE A fine quality art pottery of gray crackleware, hand decorated in cobalt-blue designs; first produced at Dedham, Massachusetts, in 1895, in innumerable flower and animal patterns, the most popular a repeating border design of rabbits

William and Mary day bed

DELFTWARE A tin-glazed earthernware first produced in Holland and England in the 17th century; often decorated to resemble Chinese porcelain, particularly the blue and white patterns of the Ming dynasty. The name "delft" was taken from the town in Holland where much of the early ware was made.

DENTILS Decorative series of rectangular, equally spaced blocks, usually projecting below a cornice. See CLASSICAL ORDER for illustration

DERRINGER A pocket-sized percussion pistol, developed after 1825 by Henry Deringer, a Pennsylvania gunsmith, who also manufactured rifles, carbines, and swords. The derringer was widely used in the South and the West; it was the weapon with which John Wilkes Booth shot President Lincoln.

DESK BOX
See BIBLE BOX

Desk-on-frame

DESK-ON-FRAME An early, simple form of the slant-front desk; in effect, the Bible box set on legs

DIAPER PATTERN Decorative effect achieved by a repeating design of lozenges, squares, diamonds, and related shapes in a diagonal pattern; used in textiles, wallpapers, inlay, and low relief carving; originally the name given to a geometric woven pattern in medieval silk fabrics

Chippendale dining table

DINING TABLE Tables designed specifically for dining first came into wide usage in America in the 1700's, in conjunction with the social and architectural concept of a room set aside exclusively for meals.

DIRECTOIRE A style of French furniture based on Greco-Roman forms and developed between 1793 and 1804 as the transitional fashion between Louis XVI styles and the Empire forms of the Napoleonic era. Directoire patterns were reflected, for example, in the designs of Sheraton and Phyfe.

DIRECTOR'S CHAIR
See CAMPAIGN FURNITURE

DISTELFINK   German for goldfinch; popularly used as the designation for all bird forms in Pennsylvania German folk art; also known as *dusselfink*, a Pennsylvania German corruption of *distelfink*

DIVAN   An upholstered sofa, with no visible framework, and usually without back or arms. The name and form originated in Turkey and Persia, where *divan*—a "council of state"—came to mean the multicushioned couch, raised on a platform, where persons of power and importance were seated. The divan was extremely popular in the late Victorian period during the craze for Near Eastern furniture designs and artifacts.

DOCUMENT DRAWER   A narrow vertical drawer set inside a desk; generally designed in pairs, one on each side of the center compartment, and camouflaged as pillarlike decorations

DOLPHIN MOTIF   The sea dolphin used as a decorative device. In American design, from the late 1700's on, dolphins reoccur in silverwork, in ormolu mounts, in dolphinlike mirror brackets, in dolphin-head feet (particularly during the Empire period), and in pressed glass, such as the dolphin candlesticks introduced by the Boston & Sandwich Glass Company and in pressed-glass epergnes and compotes with dolphin supports.

Dolphin support on pressed-glass compote

DOUGH TROUGH   Pennsylvania German; a trough in which dough was put to rise; usually set on legs and made with a flat top that served as a kneading surface; early examples often brightly decorated; also known as a dough tray

DOVETAIL A right-angled joint formed by interlocking wedges or cleats, which resemble in shape the tail of a dove

DOWEL The wooden pin or peg used to fasten two pieces of wood

DOWER CHEST A chest in which the bride's household linens, and so forth, were stored. Distinctive American types are the Hadley chest and Pennsylvania German marriage chests.

DRAKE FOOT
See TRIFID FOOT

Draped urn

DRAPED URN Carved, inlaid, or painted ornamentation of a classical urn shape draped with a simulated swag of fabric, used principally on furniture in the Federal style

DRAW TABLE A refectory-type extension table perfected in 17th-century England; the two extension leaves were drawn out from either end of the oblong table top; reproduced in America in the so-called colonial revival of the late Victorian period, although never prevalent in early American cabinetwork

DRESSER In American terminology, a chest of drawers, usually with a mirror attached. Also, in keeping with English terminology, a dresser is a type of sideboard, typically with a cupboard below and a rack of open shelves above; a forerunner of the kitchen cabinet. See also WELSH DRESSER

DRESSING BUREAU
See DRESSING CHEST

Sheraton dressing bureau

DRESSING CHEST A term first used by Chippendale for a small chest of drawers, the top drawer fitted with compartments for toilet articles or cosmetics and often made with a looking glass that folded flat into the closed drawer when not in use

DRESSING GLASS A small mirror, often on a swivel, and generally made in combination with a small set of drawers; designed to stand on top of a table or chest of drawers; first developed in England about 1700, and continuously made in varying contemporary patterns

DRESSING STAND
See DRESSING GLASS

DRESSING TABLE Any small table or stand equipped with the necessary drawers and mirror. The form that was originally known as a dressing table is now known as a lowboy, and made its general appearance at the close of the 17th century.

DROP An ornamental, turned pendant, either applied or free-hanging; in silver, the reinforcement joining the back of the bowl of a spoon and the stem

DROP FRONT
See FALL FRONT

Rococo Revival dressing table

DROP LEAF The hinged leaf of a table; when raised, it is supported by a hinged leg or arm

DRUM TABLE A round library table with drawers set under the circular top, which is often covered with an inset of tooled leather; introduced in the late 18th century

Queen Anne drop-leaf table

DRY SINK A 19th-century provincial American kitchen piece; a cabinet below, an inset sink across the top, usually lined with zinc, where a pan was set, for example, when dishes were washed

DUMB-WAITER   A movable serving stand, usually made with three or four round trays in graduating sizes mounted on a central column; designed to hold additional plates, silver, glasses, and so forth; introduced in England, early 18th century. The Chippendale style, in mahogany, was favored in America, and variations were reproduced in the colonial revival period of the late 1800's. Sometimes called a tea stand or a cake stand. Later the term was used for a lift on which dishes, food, and so forth, were passed from one floor to another.

DUTCH CARVING
See FRIESIAN CARVING

DUTCH MARQUETRY   A term often used as a general description of inlay work, because of the tradition of fine marquetry from Holland. The phrase was particularly used in the late Victorian period, when Dutch reproductions of antique inlaid furniture were extensively exported.

EAGLE   A decorative motif dating from Greek and Roman antiquities. Popularized in America through English Georgian designs of the 1700's, the eagle became doubly popular when it was designated as the national emblem, by act of the Continental Congress, in 1782. Again, as a feature of the imported French Empire style, the eagle was incorporated into American Empire designs. It has consistently appeared in carvings, textiles, mirror crestings, glassware, chinaware, whether in folk art or in highly sophisticated patterns.

Eagle supports on Empire card table

EAGLE-HEAD FOOT   Terminal of the leg of a table, sofa, or case piece carved to resemble the head of an eagle; found in American Empire styles

EARLY VICTORIAN STYLE The general term for that period of furniture design that developed around 1840 and supplanted classical revival styles of the Federal and Empire periods. Early Victorian featured eclectic elaborations of past designs, such as the Elizabethan Revival style, the Gothic Revival style, and particularly the interpretations of French baroque and rococo furniture.

Eagle-head foot

EASTLAKE, CHARLES LOCKE (1836–1906) An English designer, whose book—*Hints on Household Taste*—first published in 1868, was a best seller in England and the United States. He popularized principles of design, largely drawn from medieval sources, that stressed honesty of purpose and simplicity of form. Eastlake deplored the "sham and pretense" created by the "cheap and easy method of workmanship" in machine-made furniture. The "Eastlake Style" was a term loosely applied to furniture that actually or allegedly followed his concept of sincerity in design and construction. See also ARTS AND CRAFTS MOVEMENT

EASTLAKE STYLE The furniture fashion popular from 1870 to 1890, derived from Charles Eastlake's concepts of design; characterized by straight lines and rectangular shapes; much applied molding and trim, stylized paterae or rosettes, inset tiles, incised carving, rows of decorative spindling, and many little shelves and galleries on cupboards and bureaus and on overmantel structures

Eastlake bureau and bed

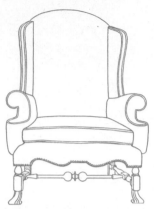

William and Mary easy chair

Eclectic Victorian chair

EASY CHAIR Any large, comfortable, upholstered chair; originally, the name given to the upholstered wing chair, introduced in the late 17th century

EBONIZE To simulate ebony by staining native wood black. In American cabinetwork ebonized decorative elements were used, for example, on court cupboards and Connecticut Valley chests of the 17th century and on various of the revival styles of the Victorian period.

ECLECTIC In furniture design the adaptation and combination of past styles, which often create—in themselves—a new style. The numerous so-called revival forms of the Victorian period were largely eclectic designs, with motifs from earlier periods freely combined at the whim of the designer.

EDDYSTONE LIGHTHOUSE CLOCK
See LIGHTHOUSE CLOCK

EDGING Thin strip of solid wood at the edge of a veneered panel, to protect the veneering

EGG-AND-DART A convex molding with an alternating design resembling an egg and a dart. See MOLDINGS for illustration

ÉGLOMISÉ
See VERRE ÉGLOMISÉ

EGYPTIAN REVIVAL STYLE A style in vogue during the first half of the 19th century, mainly in architecture, that featured such elements as pyramidal shapes, sphinx motifs, and the Egyptian leaf column—a column with stylized lotus or palm leaf patterns on the capital

ELECTROPLATED WARE
See PLATED WARE

ELIZABETHAN REVIVAL STYLE An early Victorian style, mid-19th century, characterized by ball turnings and spiral twist turnings, especially reminiscent of Cromwellian furniture of the mid 1600's. "Elizabethan," a misleading title, may well have been given to suggest the style's vaguely early English flavor. See also SPOOL FURNITURE and COTTAGE FURNITURE, derivatives of the Elizabethan Revival style

EMBOSS To create raised decorations, whether on metal, leather, fabrics, or paper

EMPIRE STYLE A massive and sumptuous style of rectilinear furniture based on ancient Greek, Roman, Etruscan, and Egyptian forms, originating in France during Napoleon's reign as emperor; popular in America from about 1815 to 1840, concurrent with Greek Revival architecture. Empire furniture is characterized by elegant severity and rich woods, with such favored elements as acanthus foliage, wreaths, animal-paw feet, eagles, stars, swags, brass mountings, and a general air of imperial triumph.

ENAMEL A decorative, vitreous glaze applied by fusion to the surface of metal, glass, or pottery

ENCOIGNURE
See CORNER TABLE

END-OF-DAY GLASS
See MARBLE GLASS

ENCAUSTIC TILE A decorative tile whose painted design is fixed to the surface by heat; used as ornament on furniture in the Eastlake style and as architectural trim

ENGRAVE To produce a pattern on a

Elizabethan Revival dressing table

Empire secretary

hard surface by incising with a graver or burin

EPERGNE   A decorative centerpiece for a dining table, usually in elaborately wrought tiered receptacles made of silver; introduced to England from France in the mid 1700's, thence to America. In the Victorian period epergnes of opaque or frosted glass were equally as popular as silver or plated ware. The word derives from the French *épargne*, a saving or treasury.

ESCUTCHEON   The decorative plate around a keyhole; derived from the earlier, heraldic meaning of a shield or coat of arms, because the escutcheon is a shield-shaped fixture

Colonial escutcheons

ESPAGNOLETTE   The head and shoulders of a female figure, used ornamentally as finials on columns or on chair and table legs — as opposed to the caryatid, a full-length female figure. The *espagnolette* was originally a French baroque and rococo motif; occasionally used on American Empire furniture and French revival forms of the Victorian era.

ÉTAGÈRE
See WHATNOT

ETRUSCAN MAJOLICA   Trade name of majolica ware made by Griffin, Smith & Hill Phoenixville, Pennsylvania, during the 1880's. See also MAJOLICA

EWER   A form of pitcher or jug, often with a wide mouth, used for pouring water or wine

F**AÏENCE**   Earthenware with ornamental designs applied in opaque, colored glazes

FAIRY LAMPS   Miniature lamps which

were designed as candle-burning night lights and were highly popular in fancy glass, "cup and cover" patterns, during the 1880's and 1890's; of English origin

FALL-FRONT The writing surface of a desk or secretary that is hinged and opens by falling forward. The first fall-front desks in America were made during the William and Mary period. Also called a drop-front

Queen Anne fall-front desk

FAN-BACK
See WINDSOR CHAIRS

FANCY CHAIRS Inexpensive, lightweight, painted chairs, in forms derived from classical revival patterns; popular from the 1790's to the 1850's; usually with cane or rush seats. Pictorial scenes were often painted on the back rail. Gold stencil work in floral and leaf designs were extensively applied to such prototypes as the Hitchcock chair.

FANCY FURNITURE An early term for any furniture painted, japanned, or stenciled with decorative designs

FANCY GLASS
See ART GLASS

FAUTEUIL French term for an upholstered chair with open arms

FAVRILE GLASS An iridescent glass developed by Louis Comfort Tiffany; produced between 1890 and 1910 in the naturalistic flowing lines of Art Nouveau; the fume blended designs, colors, and textures emanating from within the glass itself. The word "Favrile" derives from the Latin *fabrile*, meaning "handwrought."

FEATHEREDGE The edge of a board that has been thinned off, as in paneling and sheathing

Peacock Favrile vase by Tiffany

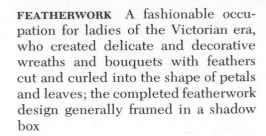

Federal gilt looking glass

FEATHERWORK A fashionable occupation for ladies of the Victorian era, who created delicate and decorative wreaths and bouquets with feathers cut and curled into the shape of petals and leaves; the completed featherwork design generally framed in a shadow box

FEDERAL STYLE (1783–1815) A general term for American furniture made in the early years of the Federal government: Sheraton, Hepplewhite, and early Empire forms. The principal motifs were acanthus leaves, swags and festoons, reeding, and lyres. Veneering and inlay were extensively used, mahogany was the fashionable wood, and the eagle was a predominant ornamentation—on finials, mirror crestings, inlay, applied brass ornaments, and so forth.

FENTON'S ENAMEL
See FLINT ENAMEL

FERROTYPE
See TINTYPE

FESTOON Painted or carved decoration in a series of loops, such as ropes of flowers and leaves; popular on Federal furniture

FIDDLE-BACK A chair back of the Queen Anne period that resembled the shape of a violin

FIELD BED A four-poster bed of light proportions, the canopy hung from an arched overhead frame; adopted from folding, portable beds intended for the field. (See also CAMPAIGN FURNITURE) Sheraton and Hepplewhite included field bed designs in their pattern manuals. The form was fashionable in America from the 1780's to the 1830's. Also called tent bed

Queen Anne fiddle-back chair

FIGURAL BOTTLES From the 1870's to the early 1900's, bottles in such shapes as fish or owls, log cabins, George Washington, or Carry Nation; used as bottling for liquor, medicine, perfume, and vinegar

FIGUREHEADS The hand-carved and painted figures on the prows of ships, made in America until the closing years of the 19th century. American patterns were generally chosen from contemporary sources: Miss Liberty, the eagle, the American Indian, presidential figures, the shipowner, his wife, or daughter. Figures from mythology or ancient history were also popular.

FILIGREE Delicate and intricate ornamental work

FINIAL A decorative device used as a terminal ornament

FIREBACK A cast-iron plate, often with a highly decorative pattern, set in the back of a fireplace to protect the masonry; first used in America from the early colonial period

FIREDOGS Andirons, particularly of a low, simple design

FIREHOUSE CHAIR A late Victorian name for a chair made in the pattern of the low-back Windsor. Inexpensive and mass produced, this type of chair was used in such public buildings as firehouses, hence its name.

FIRE SCREEN A screen, usually of tapestry, needlework, or painted wood, mounted on a supporting frame; designed to shield against the glare and heat of a fire; an elegant decorative item of the 18th and 19th centuries; made in the prevailing styles

Victorian fire screen

FLAG The rushes used for weaving chair seats; chiefly an American term. See also RUSH

FLASKS Or pocket bottles for liquor; first made with decorative designs about 1810. Patterns over the century included sunbursts, eagles, sheaves of wheat, patriotic slogans, Masonic emblems, and presidential portraits. See also FIGURAL BOTTLES

FLATWARE Flat pieces of silverware, such as knives, forks, and spoons. See also HOLLOW WARE

FLAX WHEEL
See SAXON WHEEL

FLEMISH SCROLL A reversed C- or florid S-scroll, commonly used on stretchers and chair legs of the William and Mary period

Flemish scroll

FLINT ENAMEL A ceramic formula patented 1849 by Christopher Webber Fenton, of Bennington, Vermont, that provided an improvement in the application of color to Rockingham ware. Powdered metallic oxides were dusted on a transparent glaze, the piece was then fired again, producing an enamel-like finish. Also called Fenton's enamel

FLINT GLASS Glass of a heavy, brilliant quality containing lead; also called lead glass or crystal

FLOW BLUE A Staffordshire stoneware import, introduced about 1825; a washed or clouded effect created by allowing the cobalt blue designs to "flow" during the firing; also called flowing blue

FLUTING A series of half-round, parallel furrows or channels carved into the surface of a piece of wood

Fluting

FOLIATED Ornamented with leaf forms

FONT The oil container of a lamp

FOOD SAFE A 19th-century kitchen cupboard, usually with three shelves, for storing food and baked goods; a wooden frame with metal paneling pierced in decorative patterns; chiefly midwestern. A small, one-shelved version was known as a pie safe.

Foliate

FOOT WARMER A small wooden or metal box, with a handle on top, and a metal drawer inside to hold hot coals; popular in early America as a portable stove, for such occasions as a carriage trip on a winter's day

FORM An early term for a long bench or stool

FOUR-POSTER The American term for a bed with four tall corner posts, with or without a canopy; also called a four-post bed

FRAKTUR The term used for the illuminated Pennsylvania German manuscripts done in water colors and hand lettering in the 18th and 19th centuries. Among *fraktur* illuminations were birth, baptism, and marriage certificates, Bible quotations, and house blessings decorated with folk designs of angels, birds, hearts, flowers, and so forth. About 1860 preprinted *fraktur* outlines came into use, the lettering and color filled in by hand. *Fraktur*, a contraction of *frakturschrift*, derives its name from a 16th-century German type face.

FRANKLIN STOVE The term for a decorative cast-iron, free standing fireplace derived from a stove designed by Ben Franklin in 1742; variations of the

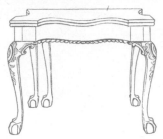

Gadrooning on Chippendale card table

Franklin stove produced to this day

FREE-BLOWN GLASS Glass formed without the use of molds, but given shape by blowing and by manipulation with hand tools

FRETWORK An ornamental design resembling latticework, either applied, freestanding, or cut in low relief; popular in the Chippendale and Federal periods and in the 19th-century revival of past styles

FRIESIAN CARVING Traditional Dutch carving of simple geometric patterns named for Friesland, a province of the Netherlands; found on artifacts of the Dutch colonial period and on Pennsylvania German work, such as spoon racks, butter molds, or salt boxes

GADROON A rufflelike ornamentation used on silver and furniture; popular as a carved edging on New York and Philadelphia Chippendale furniture

GALLERY A decorative railing, often of metal, around the edge of a piece of furniture, a shelf, or a tray

GAMING TABLES Specialized table forms for games such as chess, backgammon, or cards. See also CARD TABLE

Eclectic Victorian gaming table

GATE-LEG TABLE An early type of English drop-leaf table, made in America from about 1650; the name is derived from the gatelike structure of the legs and stretchers. When swing-leg tables came into fashionable use early in the 1700's, gate-leg tables became a provincial form.

GATHER In glassmaking, a globular mass of molten glass affixed to a blowpipe, ready to be blown

William and Mary gate-leg table

GAUDY DUTCH WARE Gaily decorated pottery extensively exported from Staffordshire between 1810 and 1830, that received its name because of its popularity with the Pennsylvania Germans

GENTLEMAN'S CHAIR Popular name for a Victorian upholstered balloon-back armchair, that was typically part of a six-piece living-room set consisting of a medallion-back sofa, a gentleman's chair, a lady's chair, and six side chairs. See also LADY'S CHAIR

Gaudy Dutch plate

GEORGIAN A term broadly used to refer to the architectural and furniture styles developed in England during the reigns of Georges I, II, and III, 1714–95. Furniture styles include late Queen Anne, Chippendale, Hepplewhite, and Sheraton.

GESSO An Italian term for plaster of Paris. In cabinetwork gesso was applied to a surface to provide a base for painting or gilding. Gilt mirror frames, for example, have a coating of gesso under the gold leaf.

GIBSON GIRL A creation of the American illustrator, Charles Dana Gibson, whose fashionable and witty drawings appeared at the turn of the century. Replicas of "the Gibson girl" were a craze of the early 1900's, on spoons, pillows, wall plaques, brooches, buttons, buckles, and on chinaware, such as a set of twenty-four black and white dinner plates produced in 1901 by the Royal Doulton Potteries, which retailed in America at fifty cents per plate.

GILT Overlay made of or resembling gold leaf, used to decorate furniture, silver, and ceramics

GINGERBREAD Popular term for jig-saw work, fretwork, filigree, and similar ornamental fancies so frequently used as decorative trim in the late Victorian period, both in architecture and in cabinetwork

GIRANDOLE Wall bracket with candle arms, often with a mirror backing. A fashionable form of girandole, introduced from France and England in the late 18th century, was backed with a circular convex or bull's-eye mirror, in a gilt frame trimmed with gilt balls and topped with an eagle. See also CONVEX MIRROR

GIRANDOLE CLOCK A wall clock, about 1815, with a round dial and round pendulum door set in gilt moldings decorated with gilt balls; so-named because of the resemblance to the girandole mirror of the Federal period

GLASS NOVELTIES
See WHIMSEY

GODDARD AND TOWNSEND A dynasty of skilled Rhode Island cabinetworkers, allied by marriage and apprenticeship, especially known for their fine furniture in the Chippendale style. The block front with shell carvings, a Rhode Island motif on such case pieces as desks and secretaries, is attributed to the creative talents of John Goddard I (1723–85) and John Townsend (1723–1809).

GONDOLA CHAIR A side chair of the late Empire period, with an arched back that curved forward to join the seat rail; adapted from a French pattern originally introduced in the Louis XV period, then reintroduced during the French Restoration, 1814–24

Empire gondola chair

GONE WITH THE WIND LAMP The

modern term for a lamp with a globular glass shade and matching font, produced from about 1880 to 1900. The popular name is anachronistic, however, coming as it does from the novel and movie, *Gone with the Wind*, set in the Civil War period.

GOTHIC CLOCK
See STEEPLE CLOCK

GOTHIC REVIVAL STYLE A style in architecture and furniture, about 1840–65, that featured pointed arches, cusps, crockets, and other motifs associated with the medieval past; not only used in home furnishings, but continuingly popular as church furniture

GOUGE CARVING Early simple carving made by chisel cuts in repeated patterns

Gothic Revival chair

GRANDFATHER CLOCK Term for a tall case clock, derived from a popular song of the 1880's, that began with the lines: "My grandfather's clock was too tall for the shelf and it stood ninety years on the floor. . . ." See also TALL CASE CLOCK

GRANDMOTHER CLOCK A modern term for a tall case clock of smaller proportions than the so-called grandfather clock

"GRAND RAPIDS" FURNITURE A loosely used term for the inexpensive, mass-produced furniture manufactured in Grand Rapids, Michigan, as well as in many other American factories from the 1850's on. The term has become more or less synonymous with "golden oak," oak finished in a very light color, that was enormously popular in mass-produced furniture at the turn of the century.

GRECIAN CROSS The X-shaped legs of

"Grand Rapids" pedestal table

Greek key motif on Empire cream pitcher

a curule chair

GREEK HONEYSUCKLE PATTERN
See ANTHEMION

GREEK KEY A repeating, geometric motif derived from ancient Greek art

GREEK REVIVAL STYLE Architecture and furnishings, from the close of the 18th century to about 1850, in which ancient Greek forms and ornamental details were dominant; furniture styles include Federal and Empire designs. The term Greek Revival, however, is especially associated with American architecture of the period, which featured classical colonnades, whether on public buildings or the front of a farmhouse.

GREEN GLASS Term for glass in its natural color, which ranges through shades of green to shades of amber; used for window glass, bottles, and so forth. Also called bottle glass

GRISAILLE Decorative painting in shades of gray that created a three-dimensional effect; from the French *gris*, or gray. In Dutch-American colonial design *grisaille*, in stylized patterns of fruits and vegetables, was popular on the Dutch *kas* — or wardrobe.

GUILFORD CHEST The name given painted chests made in the area of Guilford, Connecticut, from about 1690 to 1720; an allover painted design of stylized flowers and foliage, in lieu of carving

GUILLOCHE An ornamental motif of Greek origin consisting of a series of loosely interlacing, circular forms

GYPSY TABLE A late Victorian term for a small, lightweight table with three legs that crossed at the "knees,"

Guilloche

a fanciful name presumably derived from the three crossed poles that held a cauldron or kettle over a gypsy campfire

Hadley chest

HADLEY CHEST A colonial chest with a hinged top and usually with one or two drawers, made in and around Hadley, Massachusetts, from about 1675 to 1740, principally as dower chests; decorated with overall, incised floral designs, painted red, black, brown, or green, and often bearing the owner's initials

HAIRCLOTH A stiff, glossy, durable fabric popular in mid-19th-century upholstery, sometimes in small-figured patterns, but typically in black. The fabric was woven with the long hairs of horses' tails as the weft and with linen yarn for the warp, the width of the material necessarily limited by the length of the horsehair; many narrow-seated settees and chairs of the mid 1800's were so designed in order to accommodate haircloth as the upholstery fabric.

HAIRY-PAW FOOT A foot of a chair or any other seating form resembling the hairy paw of an animal; particularly associated with Chippendale and Empire designs

Hairy-paw foot

HAIRWORK A craze of the mid 1800's for bracelets, brooches, and other trinkets, wreaths, bouquets, and so forth that were woven from hair; generally made as a sentimental souvenir from the hair of friends and relatives, and particularly as a mourning memento of the dear departed

HALF TURNING
See SPLIT SPINDLES

HALLMARKS The symbols stamped on

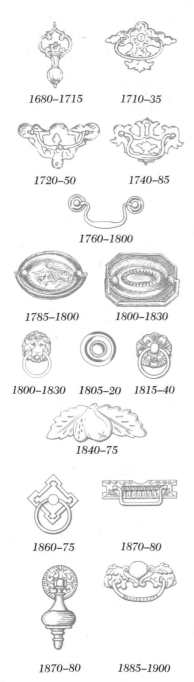

1680–1715   **1710–35**

1720–50   **1740–85**

1760–1800

1785–1800   **1800–1830**

1800–1830   1805–20   1815–40

1840–75

1860–75   **1870–80**

1870–80   **1885–1900**

Hardware: representative drawer pulls

English gold and silver to indicate the maker, the town of origin, the date, and the silver content; American silver customarily stamped with the maker's mark only

HANDKERCHIEF TABLE   A triangular drop-leaf table with a triangular single leaf, introduced in the mid 1700's. When opened, it makes a square; closed, it fits into a corner.

HARDWARE   In cabinetwork, such fittings as escutcheons, mounts, hinges, and drawer pulls

HARVARD CHAIR   A three-cornered, 17th-century American chair, with turned legs and back rails; derived from a medieval European form; named for a chair of this type still used by the president of Harvard at commencement

HARVARD LAMP
See **STUDENT LAMP**

HARVEST TABLE   A long, narrow, drop-leaf table of simple design; a 19th-century American provincial form devised to seat many people during harvest time

HAVILAND CHINA   Fine chinaware manufactured in Limoges, France, particularly for export to America. The factory was established in 1846 by David and Daniel Haviland, china importers of New York City. Continually popular in varying contemporary patterns, Haviland was especially in vogue during the 1880's and 1890's with delicate patterns of hand-painted, floral designs, the chinaware itself generally molded in delicate relief.

HEPPLEWHITE, GEORGE   (Died 1786) An English cabinetmaker whose name has become identified with the classical revival furniture catalogued in a patternbook, *The Cabinet-Maker and Upholsterer's Guide*, published by his widow in 1788. Although there is no known example of Hepplewhite's handiwork, his pattern manual offered a comprehensive view of prevailing furniture styles.

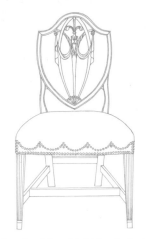

Hepplewhite shield-back chair

HEPPLEWHITE STYLE (About 1785 to 1800) The light, graceful classic revivals patterns that succeeded the Chippendale style and were characterized by square tapered legs, subtle decoration achieved by inlays, veneers, and delicate carvings. Chair backs were typically designed in shield or heart shapes. Curved façades were used on case pieces as were flaring bracket feet. The popular motifs were paterae, fans, bellflowers, wheat sheaves, urns, and medallions.

HERRINGBONE Decorative inlay composed of veneer cut obliquely and fitted together in a herringbone, or chevron, pattern

HESSIAN ANDIRONS Andirons in the shape of Hessian soldiers, walking, in partial profile; about 1790 to 1820

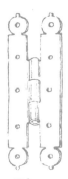

H-hinge

H-HINGE A metal hinge with long, vertical leaves held in the center by a short horizontal bar, so that the hinge, when opened, resembles the letter H

HIGHBOY The modern term for a high chest of drawers consisting of two sections: an upper case with drawers of varied depth and length; a lower case, also with drawers, set upon legs. Essentially an English form of the 1600's, it was introduced in America in the William and Mary period and was given its richest expression in the Chippendale period. Not to be confused with a tallboy, or chest-on-chest,

Queen Anne highboy

Hitchcock chair

which was set on feet rather than legs

HIRED-MAN'S BED The popular name for a narrow spool-turned bed, the mattress set on slats with no springs; mass-produced by New England and midwestern factories roughly from 1840 to 1880; designated in its time as cottage style furniture

HITCHCOCK CHAIR Mass-produced versions of the "fancy chair," about 1820 to 1860; usually painted to simulate rosewood and decorated with powdered gold stencils of fruit and flowers; first made by Lambert Hitchcock in Hitchcocksville, now Riverton, Connecticut, and widely copied in other chair factories of the period. See also FANCY CHAIR

HOBNAIL An American pressed-glass pattern, first produced about 1850 and at the height of its popularity about 1880; an overall pattern that resembled the heads of hobnails; originally called dewdrop glass, because the design was likened to drops of dew

HOLLOW WARE The term for silver forms of a hollow design such as pitchers, teapots, and creamers

HOMESPUN Home-loomed textiles; now the popular term used for handwoven coverlets

HONEYCOMB The popular name of a pressed-glass pattern, introduced about 1840, designed to look like a bee's comb

HOOKED RUG A rug, usually in colorful and elaborate patterns, made of strips of cloth or yarn drawn through a burlap backing; the loops sometimes trimmed to create a plushy effect. Hooked rugs were not widely made in

America until the 1800's.

HORN FURNITURE Furnishings made of steer, buffalo, or elk horn, popular in Europe as well as in America between 1860 and the early 1900's

HORN OF PLENTY A stylized pressed-glass pattern resembling cornucopias; also called Comet, the name by which it was originally known in the mid 1800's

HORSEHAIR
See HAIRCLOTH

Steer-horn chair

HORSESHOE SEAT A rounded chair seat with sides that curve inward as they join the back of the chair, thus creating a horseshoe shape; often used on Queen Anne chairs

Horn of Plenty bowl

HOUND-HANDLED PITCHER Pitcher with a handle formed by a stylized hound; first made in America about 1840 by Vermont and New Jersey potteries as copies of an earlier English model, in turn derived from an earlier Hungarian model. Hound-handled pitchers were widely reproduced in varying patterns of Bennington brownware—Rockingham ware—the body of the pitcher decorated in relief with hunting scenes and motifs.

Hound-handled pitcher

HUNT BOARD A form of sideboard, made chiefly in Virginia and Kentucky, beginning with the Hepplewhite period to about 1860, in varying contemporary styles. The hunt board is distinctive for its height, since it was designed as a serving table around which huntsmen could comfortably stand to enjoy food and drink.

HUNZINGER CHAIRS As manufactured in New York by George Hunzinger, in the years following the Civil War, vari-

Hunzinger chair

Hurricane shade

Inlaid Sheraton card table

ous patterns of fancy chairs, folding and reclining chairs that were representative of the contemporary vogue. Many factories produced upholstered folding chairs—an elaboration of the camp chair—or chairs whose basic lightweight design was derived from folding chairs.

HURRICANE SHADE   A cylindrical shade of glass, open at either end, designed to place over a candlestick as a protection against drafts, largely an English export item, beginning with the mid 1700's, particularly to the West Indies and the South. Early shades were clear and undecorated, with progressively elaborate designs added through the Victorian period. Also called wind glasses

HUTCH   A general term in use since the Middle Ages for a small cupboard, chest, or box, from the old French *huche*, meaning a chest or bin. Hutch table is an American term for an early colonial chair-table with storage space beneath the seat, a form that persisted in provincial manufacture into the 19th century.

I NLAY   In cabinetmaking, an ancient decorative art; a surface ornamented with insets of contrasting materials, exotic woods being most popularly used in furniture. Hepplewhite and Sheraton designs are particularly distinguished by the extensive use of inlay. The word is often generally used for marquetry, although the latter is a somewhat different technique.

IPSWICH CHEST   Oak chest of the type made in and around Ipswich, Massachusetts, about 1660 to 1680; ornamented with such carvings as arcaded panels, stylized tulip and leaf motifs, lunettes, and bands of guilloche patterns

Ipswich chest

IRIDESCENCE The interchange and mingling of colors in glass and ceramics, comparable to the play of colors seen in mother-of-pearl or soap bubbles. Iridescence was a favored quality in art glass and was most brilliantly achieved in Tiffany's Favrile glass.

IRONSTONE A durable earthenware introduced by an English patent of 1813, the early examples often decorated with blue transfer-printed designs adopted from Japanese patterns. Widely made throughout America in an almost unlimited variety of forms, ironstone as a rule is all white, sometimes with a pattern in relief.

Jacobean folding-top table

JACOBEAN STYLE From the Latin *Jacobus*, meaning James; a general term for English furniture styles introduced during the reign of James I (1603–25). Essentially an extension of Elizabethan styles, Jacobean furniture was of simple, solid construction, rectilinear in form, with carvings, turnings, and strapwork as the principal ornamentation. American colonial furniture of the 1600's is often termed Jacobean, because it was a copy of established English forms.

JAPANESE STYLE
See ANGLO-JAPANESE STYLE

JAPANNING The process of simulating oriental lacquer by the use of varnish or paint, with raised decorations created with plaster of Paris; usually in fanciful *chinoiserie* designs. The technique was introduced from England and was highly popular in America throughout the 1700's.

Japanned Queen Anne lowboy

JARDINIERE   A decorative pot or stand for plants and flowers, introduced in France toward the end of the 1700's. The name is from the French *jardin*, or garden.

JASPER WARE
See WEDGWOOD

JENNY LIND BED   Popular name for a spool bed with rounded corners on the head and foot rails; widely manufactured in America from about 1840 to 1870, and named for Jenny Lind, as were many items of spool-turned furniture, because the Swedish singer toured America at the time when such styles were at the height of their popularity.

JENNY LIND MIRROR   A dressing mirror with a cast-iron frame, again named as a tribute to the Swedish singer. The foliate frames were supported by standards representing crinolined ladies, and an American flag was attached to the center stand.

JIG SAW   A saw with a thin, vertical, reciprocating blade, used for cutting openwork patterns in wood. Throughout the Victorian era, jig-saw work was used to ornament both houses and furniture; an extremely popular amateur craze, as well, for the creation of wall brackets, hanging shelves, towel racks, wall pockets, and so forth. Also known as Sorrento work, from the fretted woodwork made in and around Sorrento, Italy

Jig-sawed scrollwork

JOINT STOOL   Or joined stool; a small, backless seat with turned legs strengthened by stretchers; so-called because the pieces were fitted or "joined" together; an English pattern widely reproduced in America during the early colonial years

Jacobean joint stool

K AOLIN
See PORCELAIN

KAS A large cupboard in the Dutch style, largely of panel construction with a heavy overhanging cornice; often painted with fruits and flowers in *grisaille*. Made in the Dutch-American colonies in and around New York from about 1680 to 1750. See also SCHRANK

Kas

KENTUCKY RIFLE An early American flintlock, derived from an earlier European model by Swiss and German gunsmiths working in Pennsylvania early in the 1700's. By lengthening the barrel and decreasing the caliber, a lighter, more accurate rifle was created. Rich inlays and engraved mountings were an embellishment added after the Revolutionary war. Because of their extensive use in the exploration and settlement of the Kentucky wilderness, these Pennsylvania firearms became known as Kentucky rifles.

KEROSENE LAMPS Lighting devices popularized after the discovery of the Pennsylvania oil fields in 1859. Kerosene, distilled from petroleum, was cleaner and better smelling than whale oil. Innumerable variations on the kerosene lamp were produced during the Victorian period ranging from the richly ornamental to the purely utilitarian; the kerosene burner was an adaptation of the earlier Argand lamp burner.

KETTLE BASE
See BOMBÉ

KEW BLAS An iridescent satin-finished art glass imitative of Tiffany's Favrile; made from about 1890 to 1910. The name was an anagram of W. S. Blake, manager of the Union Glass Works of Somerville, Massachusetts, where this type of glass was made.

Klismos chair

Kneehole Chippendale desk

KLISMOS A side chair derived from an ancient Greek type shown in vase paintings and grave monuments. The seat and rail uprights are united by a continuous line which flows into the incurved or saber leg. The klismos form was variously adapted in chair styles of the late Federal and Empire periods.

KNEADING TABLE
See DOUGH TROUGH

KNEEHOLE The center opening in a desk between the two banks of drawers; designed to accommodate the sitter's knees. The first kneehole forms made in America appeared early in the 1700's and were produced throughout the century in successive furniture styles.

KNIFE BOX A highly decorative box-case for silverware, often made in pairs and displayed on sideboards; introduced during the Chippendale period; popularly in the shape of an urn during the Hepplewhite and Sheraton periods

KNUCKLE A carved pattern resembling knuckles often used as terminals on the arms of Chippendale and Windsor chairs

KNURL FOOT
See WHORL FOOT

LACQUER In the Far East, a natural varnish from the sap of certain indigenous trees. Numerous coats of lacquer, successively dried and polished, created a hard, lustrous surface, which might be carved, inlaid, or built up in relief patterns, frequently finished in gold. The craze for lacquerwork and lacquered furniture struck the western world in the mid 1600's. See also JAPANNING, an imitative technique

LACY PRESSED GLASS A mechanically pressed glass with overall decorations in lacelike and beaded design; made in America from about 1828 to 1840, with over a thousand patterns at the height of its vogue in the 1830's. Although produced at many factories, lacy glass is particularly associated with the Boston & Sandwich Glass Company of Cape Cod, and frequently known as Sandwich glass or "lacy sandwich."

LADDER-BACK CHAIR A type of chair, with horizontal back slats resembling the rungs of a ladder, found on early simple country furniture; sometimes called a slat-back chair. In the Chippendale period the rungs were cut in curved lines.

LADY'S CHAIR A Victorian term for an upholstered, balloon-back chair, designed without arms to accommodate hoop skirts. See also GENTLEMAN'S CHAIR

LAMBREQUIN A short, often elaborately ornamental drapery on a shelf or mantelpiece or over a door or window, particularly popular in Victorian *décor*. The word derives from the Dutch *lamperkin*, a little veil.

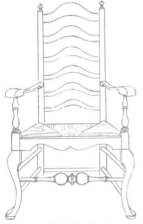

Provincial ladder-back chair

LANCET A sharply pointed arch of a window or a window light; also an arch so shaped in cabinetwork, such as the pointed arches in Gothic Revival furniture

LANTERN CLOCK A small, weight-driven wall or bracket clock, usually brass and resembling a lantern, surmounted by a bell to sound the hours; an English import of the late 17th and early 18th centuries

LATTICE Cutout, crisscross design found in highboy pediments, chair

Chippendale ladder-back chair

backs, and other furniture forms; sometimes also known as fretwork

LAZY SUSAN In American furnishings, a revolving tray for condiments set in the center of the table; a late Victorian innovation

LAZY SUSAN TABLE A circular table with a raised, circular revolving tray built into the center of the table; about 1840 to 1880; a provincial piece, chiefly of Pennsylvanian origin, frequently painted blue or dark green

LEAD GLASS
See FLINT GLASS

LEAF AND SCROLL DESIGN A serpentine acanthus leaf motif used to decorate 19th-century pressed glass

LEEDS WARE A pierced, latticework creamware widely exported from England, late 1700's and early 1800's, and popularly associated with Leeds

LEHN WARE Pennsylvania German; brightly painted woodenware, originally made in the mid 1800's by Joseph Lehn of Lancaster County, Pennsylvania

LIGHTHOUSE CLOCK An alarm timepiece, patented by Simon Willard, 1822, with a tapering wooden base suggesting a lighthouse in form and an alarm dial and bell in a glass case above. The design roughly approximated the Eddystone Lighthouse that lay off the coast of Cornwall, England.

LILY PAD In American glass the applied decoration formed by superimposing a layer of glass in a padlike form about the base of a blown-glass vessel; particularly associated with the South Jersey type of glass first produced in the late 1700's

Lighthouse clock

LIME GLASS Glass made with lime instead of lead; developed during the Civil War, when lead was scarce; a clear glass, but not so resonant or heavy as flint glass

LINCOLN DRAPE A pressed-glass pattern resembling swagged draperies, presumably inspired by Lincoln's funeral trappings

LINCOLN ROCKER A high-backed, upholstered rocking chair with open arms and a gracefully curved frame; 1860–75; so-called because a rocker of this type was owned by President Lincoln

LION-HEAD DRAWER PULL A furniture mount, usually brass or ormolu, with a ring suspended from the lion mask; used on furniture of the Federal and Empire periods. See HARDWARE for illustration

LION-PAW FOOT A foot resembling the paw of a lion, used on chairs, sofas, and case pieces, most frequently in the Empire period

LIVERPOOL POTTERY A generic name given to creamware made both in Liverpool and other Staffordshire potteries from about 1780 to 1825; particularly applied to wares with black transfer-printed decorations, often of American historical subjects

Lion-paw feet on
Empire work table

LOLLING CHAIR
See MARTHA WASHINGTON CHAIR

LONG CASE CLOCK
See TALL CASE CLOCK

LOTUS WARE The trade name for an American Belleek, a porcelainlike ware of fine quality; made from about 1890 to 1900 by Knowles, Taylor, & Knowles of East Liverpool, Ohio

Louis XIV Revival table

Louis XV Revival chair

Louis XVI Revival chair

LOUIS XIV REVIVAL STYLE A 19th-century style of furnishings imitating or recalling the large-scale, ornate, baroque forms that had been favored under the monarchy of Louis XIV. See also BAROQUE

LOUIS XV REVIVAL STYLE Mid 1800's, the style in the manner of the curvilinear, rococo fashions that characterized the Louis XV period. See also ROCOCO and ROCOCO REVIVAL STYLE

LOUIS XVI REVIVAL STYLE A 19th-century style that favored the straight lines and classical details common to furnishings originally designed during the reign of Louis XVI and revived in the 1850's by the Empress Eugénie

LOVE SEAT A latter day term for a small upholstered sofa or settee designed to seat two people, popularized in the Queen Anne period. See also CONVERSATIONAL

LOW-BACK
See WINDSOR CHAIRS

LOWBOY The American name for a side table or dressing table, as they were originally called in England. Made during the William and Mary, Queen Anne, and Chippendale periods, the lowboy—with small drawers and mounted on legs—frequently followed the design of the lower section of a matching highboy.

LOWESTOFT A small English porcelain factory, 1757 to 1802; the popular painted decorations in imitation of Chinese styles possibly explains why the Lowestoft name was applied to Chinese export wares—or East India ware—so extensively imported on American ships from 1785 to 1830. See also CHINESE EXPORT PORCELAIN

LUNETTE   A half-moon or semicircular motif; often carved, for example, in early colonial furniture of Jacobean origin; popular as an inlay on furniture of the Federal period

LUSTER WARE   Pottery with a metallic film or with decorations in silver, gold, or copper sheens. An ancient process popularized in England late in the 1700's, American manufacture began about 1824 and continued in varying contemporary styles throughout the century.

William and Mary lowboy

LUTZ GLASS
See STRIPED GLASS

LYRE   A motif representing the ancient stringed instrument; a feature of classical Greek decoration. The lyre motif was widely used in furniture of the Federal and Empire periods, for table supports and chair backs, and was particularly characteristic of Duncan Phyfe's work, the lyre carved with leaf patterns and the stringing simulated with thin brass rods.

Lyre

LYRE CLOCK   A wall or shelf clock with a lyre-shaped case; made from about 1820 to 1843 with varying decorative details in the basic pattern, chiefly by Massachusetts makers

LYRE SOFA   Descriptive term for a sofa of the Federal period, usually associated with Duncan Phyfe's work; so-called because the outward curve of the sofa's arms resembled the curved line of a lyre

MAJOLICA   A type of earthenware with a tin-enamel glaze in rich colors, first produced in America in the 1850's in imitation of English majolica. Favorite patterns included leaves, seaweed, shells, basketry, fruits, and vegetables in relief. Quantities of majolica were distributed as premiums in the 1880's by the Price Baking Powder and the Great Atlantic & Pacific Tea companies.

MAMMY BENCH
See **ROCKING BENCH**

MARBLE GLASS An opaque, purple and white pressed glass having a marbleized appearance; from about 1880 to 1905. Popularly known as end-of-day glass because it was mistakenly believed to have been made from leftovers at the end of the day's work. Also known as purple slag

MARBLEIZE To paint wood or other material in imitation of marble; a continuing mode of decoration both in interiors and on furniture, widely used in America on painted furniture of the 19th century

MARLBOROUGH LEG A leg of square section, often with a block foot, used for Chippendale chairs, tables, and other forms; the origin of the name unknown

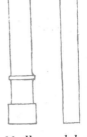

Marlborough leg

MARQUETRY A decorative veneer in which a pattern is formed by exotic woods or other choice materials (mother-of-pearl, tortoise shell, ivory, metals) and then glued to a groundwork; introduced to England from Holland in the 1600's. In American cabinetwork, marquetry was often a feature of the lavish furnishings of the "gilded age" — the post Civil War years. See also **INLAY**

MARTELÉ A special line of handmade silverware of higher than sterling quality, introduced in 1901 by the Gorham Manufacturing Company; characterized by Art Nouveau design and the unplanished hammer marks of its surfaces

MARTHA WASHINGTON CHAIR An armchair of the Federal period with tall upholstered back and open curved arms; so-named because such a chair was said to have been used by Martha Washington at Mount Vernon. Also called a lolling chair

MARTHA WASHINGTON MIRROR A colloquial name for the constitution mirror

MARTHA WASHINGTON SEWING TABLE A type of oval-shaped sewing table, often finely reeded to resemble tambour or covered with plaited silk; mounted either on four legs or on a pedestal tripod; made during the Federal and Empire periods, and so-named because Martha Washington supposedly owned a worktable of this pattern

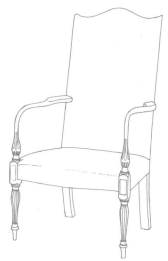
Martha Washington chair

MARY GREGORY GLASS Ornamental glassware popular in the 1870's and 1880's, the pieces hand painted in a cameo style with white enamel figures, usually of children; the name given for an artist, Mary Gregory, who worked at the Boston & Sandwich Glass Company

MASSACHUSETTS SHELF CLOCK A clock with a thirty-hour or eight-day movement of brass produced in Massachusetts from about 1800 to 1830; the basic design, a clockface mounted in a square case set upon a square pendulum case, which gave rise to such popular names as the box-on-box or the case-on-case

MASSACHUSETTS WALL CLOCK A relatively small and inexpensive clock with a light, thirty-hour movement

Massachusetts wall clock

made in the last decades of the 18th century. The square clockcase was mounted on a square pendulum case, designed to give the effect of a clock standing on a wall bracket.

MATCHSAFE A decorative container for matches, in cast iron, tin, or glass; chiefly after the Civil War, in conjunction with the wide production and sale of inexpensive, machine-made friction matches; usually in fanciful Victorian designs, made either to hang on the wall, stand on a mantel, or carry in the pocket

MECHANICAL BANK
See BANKS

MECHANIZED LAMP
See CARCEL LAMP

MEDALLION BACK An oval-shaped back of a chair or settee, resembling a medallion, popularly used in reference to the highly favored Victorian furniture design derived from Louis XV rococo styles

Medallion-back sofa

MEISSEN A German pottery known for its fine porcelains; particularly known in America for "onion pattern" chinaware, a blue and white design adapted from Chinese patterns around 1739—formalized flowers and foliage, with what had originally been peaches, but were interpreted as onions; hence, the German name *Zwiebelmuster* or onion pattern; extensively imported from the 1890's on

MEMORIAL PICTURE
See MOURNING PICTURE

MELON BULB A melon-shaped bulbous turning, of Elizabethan and Jacobean origin; in 17th-century America, typically used on table legs and the

Melon-bulb turning

supports of court cupboards

MÉRIDIENNE   A French term for a sofa or day bed of the Empire period having one arm lower than the other, with the back panel curving gracefully downward from the higher arm to the lower arm

MILK GLASS   An opaque white glass, extremely popular in the late 1800's. Pressed-glass patterns covered a host of designs, from tableware and candlesticks to animal-covered dishes and lamp bases.

MILLEFIORI   An ancient decorative device in glass, created by the fusion of many brightly colored rods of glass, which were then sliced crosswise to reveal the pattern. The cut sections, fused side by side into a bouquetlike design, were a popular motif in 19th-century paperweights. The word is Italian, meaning "a thousand flowers." See **PAPERWEIGHTS** for illustration

MISSION STYLE   A style of furniture, popular in the early 20th century, made generally of oak in simple rectilinear designs, and associated by some with the rude furnishings of early Spanish missions in California. See also **CRAFTSMAN FURNITURE** and **ROYCROFT STUDIOS**

Mission lamp

MIXING TABLE   A marble-topped table for mixing or serving drinks, as introduced in the William and Mary period. During the Federal period American mixing tables were designed with a superstructure of compartments for decanters and a tamboured roll top that closed over the marble work space. Also known as a drink table

MOCHA WARE   A mocha-colored English earthenware with bands of daubed

William and Mary mixing table

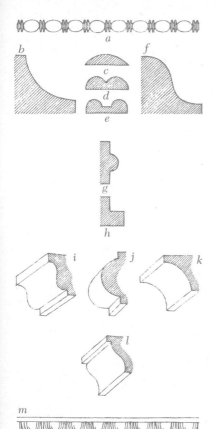

Moldings: (a) Bead-and-reel. (b) Cove. (c) Single arch. (d) Double arch. (e) Canal. (f) Cyma. (g) Astragal. (h) Fillet. (i) Cyma Recta. (j) Torus. (k) Cavetto. (l) Cyma reversa. (m) Egg-and-dart

decorations, imported from about 1830 to 1850; later copied in America

MOLDINGS Shaped decorative borders in architecture and cabinetwork

MOORISH STYLE A term interchangeable with the Turkish style of the late 19th century. See also TURKISH STYLE

MONK'S BENCH
Or Monk's table. See CHAIR-TABLE

MORRIS CHAIR An easy chair of the late 19th century, made with an adjustable back and faced with loose cushions. First produced by William Morris — architect, artist, and poet — and his associates in England in the 1860's. See also ARTS AND CRAFTS MOVEMENT

MORTISE AND TENON The method of joining two pieces of wood by inserting a tenon, or extension of one piece, into the mortise, or socket, of another; usually further secured by a pin piercing both pieces. An ancient construction technique, typically used in early American furniture of Jacobean design

MOSS ROSE A rose with mossy buds and stem, the favorite flower of the Victorians, both in the garden and in the decorative arts. Moss roses bloomed on everything, from chinaware to textiles, and in paintings, prints, stencilwork, and embroidery.

MOTE SPOON A tea table accessory introduced in England late in the 1600's; a small silver spoon with a pierced bowl and pointed handle, used to take tea leaves from the cup; the pointed handle presumably to unclog the spout of the teapot

MOTHER-OF-PEARL GLASS
See SATIN GLASS

MOUNT A piece of decorative hardware or metal ornament on a piece of furniture; bronze, brass, or ormolu

MOURNING PICTURE A needlework fashion of the early 1800's, typically embroidered with silk on a satin ground, showing an urn or monument inscribed to the deceased, with one or two figures in sorrowful attitudes beneath weeping willow trees. The Greek Revival styles of the Federal period were reflected in the dress of the women and classical form of the tomb and urn. Also called memorial picture

Morris chair

MULE CHEST
See **BLANKET CHEST**

MUNTIN The narrow wooden separations between panes of glass, whether in a window or the door of a cupboard, bookcase, or secretary; colloquially known as muttins, or mutts

Muntins in fan light

MUSTACHE CUP Late 1800's and early 1900's; a cup made with a semicircular device set inside the rim, designed to keep a gentleman's mustache from dipping into his morning coffee; sometimes with the owner's name or initials or with "Father" written across the front

NAUGHTY LADY A cast-iron bootjack of the Gay Nineties period, in the shape of a buxom lady with legs akimbo; to take off a boot, the heel was hooked between the lady's cast-iron knees. Also called Naughty Nellie

NIDDY NODDY A type of hand reel for winding newly spun yarn into hanks, resembling a double-ended anchor

NIELLO Decoration made of designs incised in metal and filled with a black metallic alloy

Norfolk latch

Ogee clock

Ogee-cross splat

NORFOLK LATCH A wrought-iron door handle and thumb latch backed with an oblong wrought-iron plate; chiefly of the 19th century. See also SUFFOLK LATCH

O **GEE**
See CYMA

OGEE CLOCK Rectangular shelf clock in a plain wooden case shaped in an ogee curve; widely made in Connecticut from about 1830 to the close of the century; also called O.G. clock

OGEE-CROSS SPLAT An open-back chair splat of the Federal period, made of two conjoining ogee or S-shaped curves

OGEE MIRROR A rectangular wall mirror, the frame shaped in an ogee curve; mahogany veneer on pine; produced in vast quantities during the Empire period

OLD BLUE
See STAFFORDSHIRE

OLEOGRAPH A type of chromolithograph printed in imitation of an oil painting, the prints often passed through an embossing machine to give a canvaslike appearance; popular in the late Victorian era

ONION PATTERN
See MEISSEN

ORMOLU From the French, meaning ground gold, used in gilding brass or bronze for the ornate mounts associated with French furniture of the 18th century. Also, an alloy of copper and zinc in imitation of gold. Ormolu ornamentations were widely used on Empire furniture and Victorian revival forms of earlier French styles. Ormolu candelabra, hung with prisms, were fashionable from about 1840 to 1860, the metal base in the shape of a Gothic cathedral or a vase of flowers or with such figures as Christopher Columbus, Jenny Lind, George and Martha Washington, Pocahontas, and so forth.

OTTOMAN An overstuffed footstool or divan, with neither back nor arms; named for the so-called Turkish fashions introduced in the 19th century. After the Civil War, a popular version of the ottoman was a richly upholstered circular couch, sometimes with a potted palm or statuette rising from its center.

Ormolu mount

OVERLAY
See **SILVER DEPOSIT**

OVERLAY GLASS Glass, popular in the 19th century, with one or more casings of differently colored glass ground away in decorative patterns revealing the underlying glass

OVERMANTEL MIRROR A mirror designed to fill the space over the mantelpiece; uncommon in America until the Federal period, when such mirrors were typically of gilded wood. In the Victorian period overmantel mirrors became elaborate architectural fancies with decorative fretwork and numerous little shelves that covered the entire chimney front.

Ottoman

OXBOW FRONT A reverse-curved front—concave in the center, convex at the ends—sometimes found, for example, on Chippendale case pieces; also called yoke front

OYSTERING Veneer showing cross-sectional grain in irregular concentric rings, resembling the shape and

Pad foot

Paperweights

markings of oyster shells; particularly favored in the William and Mary period

PAD FOOT   An oval-shaped foot used on cabriole legs, especially identified with Queen Anne styles; called a cushioned pad foot when it has a disc-shaped support or cushion underneath

PANEL-BACK CHAIR
See WAINSCOT CHAIR

PAPER FILIGREE
See QUILLWORK

PAPERWEIGHTS   Said to have first been made in France about 1820; widely produced in the United States during the Victorian period, with such popular motifs as millefiori, latticino (a lacy latticework), flowers, fruit, portraits of famous persons, and sentimental mottoes

PAPIER-MÂCHÉ   Mashed paper, molded into various shapes; an ancient Eastern technique. In the early Victorian period, papier-mâché—japanned, painted with floral designs, and inlaid with mother-of-pearl—was extremely popular for clockcases, small tables, side chairs, sewing boxes, trays, fire screens, snuff boxes, music stands, and similar pieces.

PARIAN WARE   Fine-grained, unglazed porcelain resembling Parian marble, first made by the Copeland works in England in the 1840's. First produced in America, after 1850, by Christopher W. Fenton in Bennington, Vermont. Used for statuettes, pitchers, vases, trinket boxes, and tableware; occasionally with color, such as the blue and white associated with the potteries in Bennington; noted for delicate appliqués of grape clusters, with leaves and tendrils. Also called statuary ware

PATCHWORK QUILT   A uniquely American type of bedquilt, developed during the colonial period when material was scarce. Odd scraps of fabric, sewn together, lined, and quilted, at first a utilitarian type of handiwork, became a highly decorative craft early in the 1800's with the appearance of the fanciful and intricate geometric designs, now typical of American patchwork quilts. See also CRAZY QUILT

PATERA   A flat, circular ornament resembling the saucers, or paterae, used by ancient Romans for libations; usually used in low relief as a decorative motif in architecture or furniture in classical revival fashions, such as Hepplewhite and Sheraton, and extensively in various Victorian revival forms

Patera

PATINA   The color or finish of bronze, copper, or wood surfaces resulting from age or use

PATINATE   To produce an artificial patina on wood or metal

PATTERN GLASS   A term for pressed glass produced in sets, the different pieces of which carry the same pattern; also called pattern ware

PATTERN MOLD   A mold, with depressions or protuberances forming patterns on the interior surface, into which glass is forced or blown, then removed and expanded

PAUL REVERE LANTERN   The popular but mistaken name for an early 19th-

Paul Revere pitcher

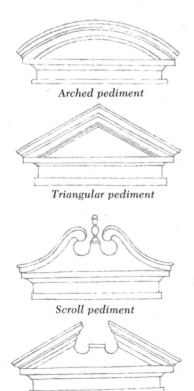

Arched pediment

Triangular pediment

Scroll pediment

Broken pediment

century farm lantern: cylindrical in shape, of pierced tin, with a conical top

PAUL REVERE PITCHER Popular name for a handsome pitcher of simple design, widely copied to this day from a silver pitcher made by Paul Revere, the colonial silversmith, who had adapted his design from a Liverpool pottery pitcher

PEACHBLOW A type of art glass introduced in the late 1880's; colored and shaded to simulate Chinese porcelain with a "peach bloom" glaze

PEACOCK MOTIF An element of design resembling a peacock or its feathers used by Art Nouveau artists, especially Tiffany, whose Favrile glass was noted for peacock colors and motifs. Bouquets of peacock plummage were a fashionable ornamental touch in late Victorian *décor.*

PEAR-DROP HANDLE Furniture hardware, typical of the William and Mary period; a patterned brass backplate and a pull shaped like a teardrop or pear. A larger version with a wooden pull was used on Eastlake pieces of the Victorian period. See HARDWARE for illustrations

PEDESTAL TABLE A table, usually round or oval, supported by a single central column with spreading feet, designed primarily as dining and card tables; popularized early in the 1800's through Duncan Phyfe's interpretation of a Sheraton pattern; continuingly produced in varying shapes, sizes, and contemporary styles

PEDIMENT In architecture, a triangular or arched section above the entablature; in cabinetmaking, a similar top, either straight, or curving, for case pieces; a distinctive feature in the Chippendale period

PEEL A long-handled shovel for removing cooked food, such as loaves of bread, from a brick oven; from the Latin *pala*, or shovel

PEG LAMP
See WHALE-OIL LAMP

PEMBROKE TABLE A small, rectangular drop-leaf table with a drawer, the leaves supported by hinged brackets in the frame; introduced in the Chippendale period and widely produced in the Federal period; the name attributed to an Earl of Pembroke, said to have originated the design

PENCIL-POST BED Popular name for a four-poster bed of "country" origin; the thin posts, designed to hold a canopy, shaped with six sides, like a pencil; late 18th and early 19th centuries

Federal pembroke table

PENNSYLVANIA GERMAN The furniture and artifacts made between the early 1700's and the mid 1800's by German, Dutch, and Swiss settlers in southeastern Pennsylvania. European folk designs were perpetuated in their furniture forms, wood carvings, pottery, metalwork, and brightly painted decorations. Hearts, tulips, birds, animals, and geometric designs were favorite motifs. Popularly called Pennsylvania Dutch. See also DISTEL-FINK, FRAKTUR, KENTUCKY RIFLE, LEHN WARE, and SCHRANK

Pennsylvania German chest

PEWTER An alloy chiefly consisting of tin hardened with varying amounts of antimony, copper, or bismuth with lead as a substitute for copper in soft, common pewter; shaped either in molds or hammered over a form. Early colonial production was limited by the British tax on tin, and worn pewter was generally melted down and recast. The majority of extant American pewter dates roughly from 1750 to 1850, when it was supplanted by inexpensive crockery and glassware. See also BRITANNIA WARE

Duncan Phyfe sofa

PHYFE, DUNCAN (1768–1854) Scottish-born American cabinetmaker, who worked in New York City from about 1792. His finest work was done in the Sheraton style, the graceful and elegant designs ornamented with such carved motifs as reeding, swags of bow-knotted, tasseled draperies, and stylized leaf patterns. The lyre motif and pedestal table are especially associated with his name, which has come to be used as a synonym for Sheraton designs of the Federal period, although many excellent cabinetmakers worked in the same style. Phyfe's later pieces in the Empire mode, after 1820, lack the quality and beauty of his early work.

Pie-crust Chippendale table

PIECRUST TABLE A tripod table of the Chippendale period; the circular top has a scalloped "piecrust" rim; usually of tilt-top construction

PIERCING On furniture, any open-work carving, such as the open patterns on a chair back; in metalwork, an open design created by cutting away the metal

PIER TABLE A table designed to stand against a pier, that section of a wall between two windows or doors, usually beneath a pier glass; a side table. An elegant European innovation of the 18th century, introduced in America in the early 19th century. See

also CONSOLE TABLE

PIE SAFE
See FOOD SAFE

PILASTER A rectangular or half-round pillar on the surface of a piece, in imitation of the architectural pilaster or engaged pier that projects slightly from the wall; typically in the pattern of classical columns; popular, for example, on Chippendale case pieces and on forms of the Federal period

Empire pier table

PILGRIM FURNITURE A term for early American furniture, from about 1650 to 1690, patterned in the Jacobean styles of 17th-century England. See also JACOBEAN STYLE

PILLAR AND SCROLL FURNITURE An Empire style of the 1830's and 1840's; the first widely produced machine-made furniture and characterized by sturdy, flat-sided scroll or S-supports and pillars in simple, strong patterns; typically in mahogany or mahogany veneer

PILLAR AND SCROLL SHELF CLOCK Latter-day name for the first successfully mass-produced American shelf clock, put into manufacture about 1816 by Eli Terry of Connecticut, with subsequent variations by other clockmakers until about 1840. The case stands on slender feet, with pillars up the sides, and a broken-arch pediment or double scroll at the top; commonly, with thirty-hour wooden works.

Empire scroll-support table

PINEAPPLE MOTIF The symbol of hospitality, often carved over early American doorways; in the early 1800's, a popular motif on furniture, such as the carved finials on four-poster beds

PIONEER
See WESTWARD HO

Pillar and scroll shelf clock

Plank chair

PLANISHING Light hammering of metal to produce a smooth surface

PLANK CHAIR A chair of medieval design, first made in colonial America by settlers from northern Europe, particularly those with a Germanic folk tradition. The chair is made with plank seat and stick legs, the back often carved in peasant designs.

PLATE Term used for forms made of solid silver or gold of sterling or standard quality

PLATED WARE Forms made of a thin layer of silver over a heavier base of copper or other metals; manually fused on Sheffield plate, an English technique from the 1740's to the mid 1800's; chemically electroplated from the 1840's on, in what became one of America's leading 19th-century industries

PLATEAU A long, low decorative centerpiece for the dining table, generally of a gilt-bronze or silver, mounted on short feet or a plinth, very much in vogue for fashionable table settings in Boston, New York, and Philadelphia during the second half of the 18th century. Usually made in several short pieces so that its length could be adjusted, the plateau was designed to display table decorations. In France, also called a *surtout*

PLATFORM ROCKER An upholstered rocking chair, usually in the Eastlake style, invented about 1870; the body of the chair attached to a platform by yoke springs; sometimes manufactured as part of a parlor set. Also called a patent rocker

POMONA An art glass, first produced in 1885, the frosted ground etched

Eastlake platform rocker

with floral, berry, or vine patterns in yellow; a band of amber at the rim

PONTIL An iron or steel rod which holds hot glass for finishing after it has been blown; also called a punty

PONTIL MARK The mark on a piece of blown glass where it was attached to the pontil; also called punty mark

PONTYPOOL
See TINWARE

PORCELAIN From the French word for the Venus shell. True hard-paste porcelain, which originated in ancient China, is a mixture of rare clays, kaolin (china clay) and petuntse (china stone), fired at high temperatures to produce a vitrified, translucent body. The secret of hard-paste porcelain was discovered in Europe in 1708 at the Meissen works. In America, despite early attempts, it was not successfully produced until 1825, when porcelain was briefly manufactured by William E. Tucker of Philadelphia. The next successful American production was Parian ware, introduced in the 1840's.

PORRINGER A shallow bowl in silver or pewter, with a flat, pierced handle; associated with colonial American design. The porringer, now thought of as a child's dish, was made in several sizes as a bowl for porridge (or pottage), which originally was any sort of soup or stew thickened with meal.

Porringer

POUNCE BOX
See STANDISH

PRANG, LOUIS Founder of Louis Prang & Company, Boston, Massachusetts, one of America's most successful producers of popularly priced chromolithographs and greeting cards during

the latter half of the 19th century

PRESS CUPBOARD   Similar to the court cupboard, but with both the lower and upper sections containing drawers or storage space with doors; 17th-century Jacobean design

PRESSED GLASS   Glass whose shape and decoration are formed by being mechanically pressed in a mold; a process introduced in the 1820's and credited as an American innovation. Over two thousand five hundred patterns and variants have been listed for the 19th century.

PRINCE OF WALES FEATHERS   Decorative motif of carved or painted feathers, sometimes set within an oval chair back in the Hepplewhite style of the Federal period; commonly associated with the insigne of the Prince of Wales

Prince of Wales feathers

PRINTED WARE   Pottery decorated with transfer-printed designs, an inexpensive substitute for hand-painted decoration. Printed English pottery, such as Staffordshire and creamware, was not imitated in the United States until the 1830's.

PUNCHED WORK   Decoration, in relief, wrought by closely set dots punched into metal or wood; particularly associated with provincial designs in traditional folk patterns

PURPLE SLAG
See MARBLE GLASS

Q **UATREFOIL**   A stylized decoration with four lobes or leaves; a Gothic and Gothic Revival motif

QUEEN ANNE STYLE   The furniture style introduced in England during the reign of Queen Anne (1702–14);

Quatrefoil

fashionable in America from about 1720 to 1750, though elements of the style persisted in provincial cabinet-work. Queen Anne furniture is characterized by the lightness of its lines, the accentuation of curves, the appearance of the cabriole leg (often with scallop shells carved on the knees), and the extensive use of walnut, both in solids and veneers.

QUEEN'S BURMESE WARE
See BURMESE

QUEEN'S WARE
See CREAMWARE

QUEZAL GLASS An iridescent art glass introduced about 1917, in imitation of Tiffany's Favrile glass

QUILLING Ribbon of glass applied and pinched into wavy lines; also called pinched trailing

QUILLWORK In the decorative arts, a fashionable hobby among English and American ladies of the 17th and 18th centuries. Narrow, rolled slips of paper were colored, gilded, and twisted into ornamental patterns, often with mica, shells, or metal threads, for the decoration of such items as mirror frames, boxes, or sconces; sometimes called paper filigree. Quillwork is also the term for decorative patterns on skins or fabrics created from porcupine quills by certain North American Indian tribes.

RAT-TAIL An ornamental reinforcement, resembling a tail, on the underside of the bowl of a spoon; introduced on late 17th-century English silver

RAT-TAIL HINGE An early hinge of medieval design with a tapered, curved extension running downward,

Queen Anne open armchair and tea table

Rat-tail hinge

Reed music stand

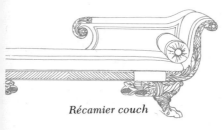

Récamier couch

Reeding

usually with a cutout decoration at the end

RATTAN A type of palm whose stem (either the outer casing called cane or the inner pith called reed) is suitable for making furniture of intricate patterns. Originally imported during the early days of the China trade, rattan furniture was widely produced in America after the Civil War in lavishly ornate Victorian designs. See also **WICKERWORK**

RAYO LAMP A kerosene lamp of utilitarian design, typically with a nickel-plated font and stand and a green glass tam-o'-shanter or umbrella shade

RÉCAMIER A day bed or couch of the Empire period, originally without a back, the head and foot scrolled outward. Its name came from the portrait of Juliette Récamier by Jacques Louis David, in which the lady reclined on a couch of this type. The form was derived from an ancient Roman couch. See also **MÉRIDIENNE**

REDWARE Early American pottery, particularly associated with New York, New Jersey, and Pennsylvania; made from a local clay that turned red-brown in firing; popularly decorated with slip patterns or with sgraffito and produced by local potters well into the 19th century. American Indian pottery was also made of this type of clay.

REEDING A motif, in semicircular relief, resembling straight, stylized reeds; a characteristic carving on furniture in the Sheraton style

REGENCY An English classical revival style, roughly from 1810 to 1820 when the Prince of Wales acted as regent for his father, George III.

Greek, Roman, and Egyptian motifs and forms were featured, as in the French Empire styles, although in a modified manner.

RELIEF Decoration that is raised above the surface, whether on metal, ceramics, or glass, or wood

RENAISSANCE REVIVAL STYLE A Victorian furniture fashion, popular in the 1860's and 1870's, influenced by the revival in France of 16th-century forms and motifs. The Renaissance style is characterized by stiff and heavy outlines, elaborated with crestings, pediments, cartouches, applied medallions, flower and fruit motifs, and trophy swags—all heavily carved and in high relief.

REPOUSSÉ Designs in metal raised on a surface by hammering from the back; particularly associated with elaborate relief patterns popularized in 19th-century silver

Renaissance Revival armchair and table

RESTORATION CHAIR A William and Mary chair, a caned seat and a tall back with a caned panel; richly ornamented with carved scrolls and leaf foliage. English designs often included a crown in the ornate cresting. The chair was named in honor of the restored monarchy—Charles II's return to the throne in 1660.

RETABLOS Pictures of holy persons or objects painted on wood panels over a gesso ground, a provincial religious art of Mexico and New Mexico (now New Mexico, Arizona, Colorado, and Texas) principally from about 1750 to 1850. See also SANTOS

RIBBAND BACK CHAIR The contemporary name given to a Chippendale design in which the pierced chair back

Restoration chair

is carved in a pattern of interlaced ribbons. Ribbon motifs, painted or carved, were featured in French and English rococo decorations of the late 17th and 18th centuries.

RIBBON GLASS A striped pattern, usually in alternating clear and frosted ribbon stripes, variously used in pressed-glass patterns

Rinceau

RINCEAU Ornamental motif of elaborate scrollings and leaves, usually in a symmetric design; a recurring decorative motif derived from classical sources

ROCKING BENCH A bench or settee of Windsor spindled construction, made with rockers and a detachable spindled gate, or railing, that extends across a section of the seat; often painted and gold stenciled. An American provincial pattern, from the early 1800's to about 1860, it was designed so a baby could lie on the seat without rolling off; the mother or nurse could sit alongside and rock — while attending to such chores as sewing. Also known as a mammy bench and a cradle rocker

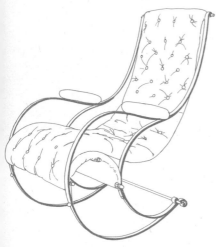

Metal-frame rocker

ROCKING CHAIR Any chair made to rock back and forth; an immediate national favorite from its introduction in the 1700's; now considered, in fact, to be typically American. Early rockers were basically ladder-back or Windsor chairs with rockers attached, from which evolved the distinctive Boston and Salem rockers. In the Victorian era numerous new designs were developed, such as the upholstered rocker, bentwood rockers, bent metal-framed rockers (called "digestive chairs" by some manufacturers), and

the platform rocker. See also BOSTON
ROCKER, LINCOLN ROCKER, PLAT-
FORM ROCKER, and SALEM ROCKER

ROCKINGHAM WARE
See BENNINGTON WARE

ROCOCO A style of art and decoration
that evolved in 18th-century France
and supplanted the grandeur of the
baroque period. Rococo, from which
Chippendale drew many of his designs, is characterized by curvilinear
patterns, a light and graceful feeling,
with a profusion of asymmetric ornamentation mingling leaf, flower, shell,
and scroll forms. The name is derived
from the rocks *(rocailles)* and shells
(coquilles) that provided elaborate,
artificial decorations in French
gardens.

ROCOCO REVIVAL STYLE A style
popular in the middle decades of the
19th century, which freely interpreted
French designs of the first half of the
18th century; characterized by S- and
C-curves, scrolls, and shell and
floral carvings. See also BELTER,
JOHN and LOUIS XV REVIVAL STYLE

ROGERS GROUPS Mass-produced
plaster statuettes designed by the
American sculptor, John Rogers
(1829–1904); from 1860 to the end of
the century, one of the most popular
items of Victorian *décor*. Rogers' subjects included Civil War themes,
historical figures, and everyday scenes
from American life.

*Rococo Revival cast-iron
mirror and table*

ROLL-TOP DESK Any desk with a top
that rolls up into the frame of the
desk; either a cylindrical solid cover,
as introduced in France in the 18th
century, or a tambour construction
(strips of wood glued to canvas) as

Rookwood coffeepot

popularized in the Hepplewhite period. Now, popularly, a roll-top is the sturdy golden oak desk mass produced in the late 1800's and early 1900's.

ROOKWOOD POTTERY Founded in Cincinnati in 1880, the outgrowth of a ladies' china painting class and yet another manifestation of the Arts and Crafts movement. Rookwood was possibly the most influential art pottery of its day, specializing in one-of-a-kind, hand-thrown ceramics and was noted for rich underglaze colors and Japanesque forms and motifs.

ROPE BED Any early bedstead in which the mattress was supported on a network of rope, the rope either threaded through holes in the bed rails or wound around small knobs affixed to the rails. Wooden rope wrenches or "keys," often carved with fanciful provincial designs, were used to tighten the rope webbing. Slat beds with springs did not become commonplace until after the 1820's.

ROSE MEDALLION A popular Chinese import from about 1812 to the closing years of the century; green enameled chinaware with medallions of pink flowers, birds, butterflies, or Chinese figures. Also known as Rose Canton

ROSETTE A decorative motif with a stylized flower set within a circle, square, or elipse; of ancient origin used on classical revival styles of the 19th century

ROSEWARE English chinaware, a popular export from about 1815 to 1860; stylized rose motifs in warm colors and bold patterns, imitative of earlier Japanese porcelain and marketed as "gaudy ware" for the provincial trade

ROUNDABOUT CHAIR
See CORNER CHAIR

ROYAL FLEMISH A late 19th-century art glass; oriental designs in raised gold outlines against a matte ground of beige and russet tones; Mount Washington Glass Company, New Bedford, Massachusetts

ROYCROFT SHOPS An arts and crafts establishment founded in 1895 in East Aurora, New York, by Elbert Hubbard, which specialized in hand-crafted pottery, leatherwork, metalwork, and furniture in the Mission style; the latter adapted from Gustav Stickley's Craftsman furniture

RUSHLIGHT An ancient and primitive lighting device. Fat-soaked rushes were burned in an iron clip mounted either on a wooden or iron tripod base; used into the 19th century on the frontier.

RUSH SEAT A chair or settee seat made of rushes or reeds, twisted and tightly woven; an ancient technique of continuing popularity, now largely done with simulated rush. Also known as a flag seat

Rush seat on provincial chair

RUSTIC STYLE Furniture made with rustic designs of tree branches was a fashionable English novelty in the mid-18th century. In Victorian America, the rustic theme — twigs, branches, bark, leaves, and vines — was variously interpreted in silverware, ceramics, furniture (both in wood and cast iron), on picture and mirror frames, and architecturally in such structures as rusticated summer houses for the garden.

Rustic table

Saber legs on Empire chair

Salem secretary

S **ABER LEG** A narrow curved leg resembling the shape of a saber; copied from the Greek klismos and used on Federal and Empire chairs and sofas

SADDLE SEAT A shaped wooden seat with a central ridge at the front, vaguely resembling a saddle; common to Windsor chairs

SALEM ROCKER An armless, slightly smaller version of the Boston rocker; designed as a lady's rocking chair

SALEM SECRETARY A Sheraton secretary-bookcase; the upper section with two or four glazed doors; the projecting lower section fitted with drawers, the center drawer a fall-front writing compartment; so-named because of its association with cabinetwork of the Salem area in the Federal period

SALT GLAZE A hard, rough, transparent glaze on earthenware or stoneware, produced by rock salt thrown into the kiln at the height of firing

SAMPLER Originally, the samples of various embroidery stitches. By the 1700's samplers were generally the work of young ladies, as a demonstration of the stitches they had mastered. The form was quickly adapted into patterns suitable for framing, with the alphabet, poetry, Biblical quotations, little landscapes with figures, and sentimental mottoes—usually embroidered in simple cross-stich on linen. After the 1830's, the custom of making samplers gradually died out.

SANDWICH GLASS A general term for early pressed glass made at the Boston and Sandwich Glass Company, founded in 1825 at Sandwich on Cape Cod. The term is sometimes erroneously used to refer to any American pressed glass, especially of the lacy variety.

SANTEROS Makers of *Santos*. See also SANTOS

SATIN GLASS A late 19th-century art glass with a satin-matte finish and an opaque lining. Mother-of-pearl glass was a variation with a highly lustrous finish, the inner core with its diamond, swirl, and herringbone patterns covered with a transparent overlay.

SANTOS From the Spanish *santo*, meaning saint; images of holy persons or objects, such as a cross, done in a variety of media—stone, wood, metal, plaster, painted or printed pictures. Made in the Spanish colonial Southwest, principally from about 1750 to 1850. The maker of a *santo* is called a *santero*. See also BULTOS and RETABLOS

SAWBUCK A table with X-shaped supports, of a type prevalent in Gothic patterns of northern Europe. The earliest American examples from the 17th century were chiefly of Swedish origin among settlers in the Delaware Valley. The pattern spread quickly as a rustic, country table and is still being produced.

Sawbuck table

SCHOOLMASTER'S DESK A slope-front, boxlike desk mounted on long legs; made throughout the 1800's in varying simple patterns; extensively used both in the classroom and in business offices

SCHRANK The Pennsylvania German name for a large wardrobe comparable to the Dutch *kas;* early 1700's to mid 1800's

SCONCE From an old French word

meaning a lantern; a wall bracket fitted with one or more candlesticks; in wide use since the Middle Ages and made over the centuries in metal, gilded wood, with needlework panels, or mirrored backplates, and so forth

SCRATCH CARVING   The simplest form of incised carving, done in plain, single line patterns; early colonial and in later provincial work

SCRIMSHANDER
See SCRIMSHAW

SCRIMSHAW   American nautical slang of unknown origin for objects carved from whale teeth and whalebone in decorative shapes and patterns, the engraved designs often filled with rubbings of ink or other dark pigments; made by American seamen in the 18th and 19th centuries; also called scrimshander

Scrimshaw

SCROLL   A spiral or rolled decoration; C- and S-scrolls were a favorite baroque and rococo motif

SCROLL PEDIMENT   A broken pediment formed by two S or cyma curves; usually with a carved ornament (such as an urn or a spiral flame) mounted between the scrolls. A baroque design of classical origin extensively used on Queen Anne and Chippendale case pieces. Also called swanneck pediment. See PEDIMENT for illustration

SECRETARY   A double-bodied case piece, the bottom section a fall-front desk, the upper section a bookcase or cabinet; introduced during the William and Mary period. The secretary was a continuing favorite in successive furniture styles through the 1800's.

William and Mary secretary

SERPENTINE FRONT   In cabinetwork,

an undulating curve, convex or rising in the center, and concave or inward on either side; popular, for example, in Hepplewhite designs, such as the front of a chest of drawers or a sideboard; the opposite of an oxbow front

SETTEE A small sofa; the word, which first appeared in English inventories early in the 1700's, usually connoted a light, openwork frame, with caned seat and back or with spindles. Upholstered settees were not widely made in America until the Chippendale and succeeding Federal periods.

SETTLE A long seat or bench of Gothic origin, with arms and a high, solid wooden back as a protection against drafts; 17th- and 18th-century American, often with a chest under the hinged seat

SEWING BIRD A metal sewing accessory, popularly in the shape of a bird and designed to be clamped on the edge of a table; used throughout the 19th century to facilitate such needlework as hemming. One end of the material was held in the bird's beak, which operated on a spring mechanism and held the material taut.

SEWING TABLE
See WORK TABLE

SGRAFFITO The design on pottery made by cutting or scratching through the outer glaze to expose the color of the clay beneath; traditional in European peasant pottery and associated in American ceramics with the Pennsylvania German redware. Sgraffito is from the Italian verb *sgraffiare*, to scratch.

SHAKER FURNITURE Furniture made

Serpentine chest of drawers

Queen Anne settee

Shaker tripod stand

in the communal workshops of the Shakers, a religious sect who founded independent, self-sustaining villages from Maine to Indiana. From the 1790's through the 19th century, their furniture forms remained basically unchanged: functional, provincial patterns, distinguished by fine craftsmanship, balanced proportions, a lack of decorative detail, and overall exquisite simplicity of form.

SHAVING MUG Popular in the Victorian period, a mug in which shaving lather was mixed; usually kept on display at the neighborhood barber shop and marked with the owner's name or monograms, and often with decorations illustrating the owner's occupation.

SHAVING STAND As popularized in the early 1800's, a small table or stand, fitted with a swivel mirror and mounted on long legs or a single pedestal at the proper height for a gentleman to stand before the mirror while shaving; made throughout the century in varying contemporary fashions

SHEAF OF WHEAT
See WHEAT

SHEFFIELD PLATE
See PLATED WARE

SHELL MOTIF The scallop shell, an ancient and recurrent decorative motif; predominant in French rococo designs and widely adopted in the Queen Anne period. In American Chippendale forms, the shell is especially associated with the block-front carvings of the Rhode Island school. On silverware, the shell is a motif of continuing popularity.

*Shell motif on
Chippendale lowboy*

SHELLWORK In the decorative arts, a

fashionable handiwork for ladies of leisure, particularly during the Victorian era when tiny sea shells were used to create a host of ornamental delights — bouquets of flowers, trinket boxes, picture frames, jewelry, and shell mosaic landscapes with figures

SHERATON, THOMAS (1751–1806) English cabinetmaker and designer, whose name has become synonymous with the classical revival styles published in his pattern manuals: *The Cabinet-Maker and Upholsterer's Drawing-Book* (1790) and *The Cabinet Dictionary* (1803). Sheraton, who was also a Baptist lay reader, lived in obscurity and poverty, eking out a meager living for himself and his family as a drawing master. As in the case of his contemporary, George Hepplewhite, there are no known examples of Sheraton's cabinetwork. His fame rests entirely on his pattern books of furniture fashions.

Sheraton fancy chair

SHERATON FANCY Popular name for a type of turned, painted, wooden side chair; about 1800 to 1820; typically with tapered front legs that turn out slightly at the base with small knob feet; a rush seat, rounded in front; the back shaped with a slight backward curve and several rows of delicate horizontal splats with little balls between the rows (a motif repeated on the front stretcher) and a straight-line, rectangular top rail with stenciled decorations

SHERATON STYLE (1800–1820) A light, elegant, classical revival style, characterized by straight lines, slender tapering legs, square chair backs, and a pronounced use of reeding as a deco-

Sheraton square-back chair

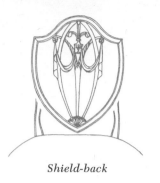

Shield-back

rative element. Ornamentation included delicate inlay work and carving in light relief of such prevailing classical motifs as urns, festoons, sprays of foliage, wheat ears, paterae and stylized leafage.

SHIELD-BACK CHAIR A chair of the Federal period with an open back in the shape of a shield, filled with such designs as Prince of Wales feathers, swags and ribbons, vase forms, and so forth; particularly associated with Hepplewhite patterns

SIDEBOARD A specialized dining-room piece for storage and serving, fitted with drawers and cupboards beneath a table top. The form evolved in England late in the 1700's and was introduced to America in the Hepplewhite style about 1785.

SIDE CHAIR A general term for a chair without arms, usually small, lightweight, and easily moved. The origin of the term is uncertain, although it has been suggested that the name was given because such chairs were used at the side of the dining table, as opposed to the armchair which traditionally stood at the head of the table.

SILHOUETTE A profile or figure cut from black paper, or cut out of a white background and faced with black paper; a type of portraiture popular in America from the late 1700's to the mid 1800's, practiced by professional artists (often itinerant) and amateurs alike. The name is derived from a French government official of the mid 1700's, Étienne de Silhouette, noted for his stringent economies; anything inexpensive, therefore, was known as a silhouette. The word was ultimately given to inexpensive "profiles" or "shades," as the black cutouts were originally called.

SILVER DEPOSIT An overlay of silver electrochemically deposited on glass, pottery, and other materials in ornamental, openwork designs; a popular technique of the 1890's and the early 1900's for vases, perfume bottles, decanters, and other such items

Silver deposit vase

SILVERED GLASS Glass in which a deposit of silver is encased between covering layers of clear glass; introduced by the New England Glass Company in the 1850's

SINUMBRA LAMP
See ASTRAL LAMP

SIX-BOARD CHEST Popular name for a storage chest or blanket chest made of six boards—the top, the bottom, and the four sides

SKIRT
See APRON

SLAT-BACK CHAIR
See LADDER-BACK CHAIR

Slat-back chair

SLEEPY HOLLOW CHAIR An upholstered version of the gondola chair, about 1850 to 1870; so-named because such a chair was a favorite of Washington Irving, author of *The Legend of Sleepy Hollow*

SLEIGH BED The American name for an Empire style bed, the headboard and footboard of equal height and curving outward in a form similar to the front of a horse-drawn cutter or sleigh; popular from about 1820 to 1850

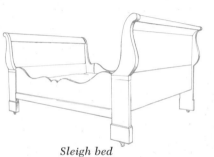

Sleigh bed

SLIPPER CHAIR The American name for a side chair, usually upholstered, and set on low legs so slippers and other footgear could be easily put on and taken off. Introduced in America in the Queen Anne period, typically with a high narrow back and simple lines until the Victorian era, when a variety of little overstuffed bedroom chairs were popularized as slipper chairs

SLIPPER FOOT A slim, elongated pointed foot; Queen Anne period

Slipper foot

SLIPPER STOOL A stool with a hinged lid, usually upholstered, over a compartment for slippers; introduced about 1840; also called slipper box

SLIP WARE Red earthenware decorated by the application of colored slip (diluted clay) to the glazed surface; a popular ornamental technique on Pennsylvania German ceramics to the mid 1800's

Snake foot

SNAKE FOOT A foot resembling the head of a snake; a Queen Anne pattern also used on tripod tables of the Chippendale period

SOLAR LAMP A modified Argand lamp of the 1840's and 1850's; designed for burning lard oil. Typically, the standard was a brass column on a marble base; above, a glass globe was hung with prisms.

SORRENTO WORK
See JIG SAW

SOUTH JERSEY GLASS A general term for free blown glass with traditional decorations — the lily pad, threading, quilling, or prunts (blobs of applied glass); the name derived from the 18th-century patterns produced at the Wistar glass factory in southern New Jersey. Such free-blown pieces were made by workers in numerous factories up to the 1870's, sometimes as a commercial venture, but usually as gifts for family and friends.

SOUVENIR SPOONS A late Victorian fad; silver or silver-plated spoons decorated with commemorative emblems, historical figures, buildings, and views of scenic attractions

SPADE FOOT The foot of a tapering, square-section leg, somewhat wider than the leg itself, in profile suggesting a spade; often used in Federal designs

Spade foot

SPANISH COLONIAL STYLE Furniture made in the Southwest, up to about 1840, in primitive interpretations of Spanish Renaissance styles and created with basic hand tools, mortise-and-tenon, dovetail, and dowel construction; solid, rectangular lines, with simple carvings, grillwork made from hand-shaped spindles, and painted decorations in traditional Spanish-Mexican designs

SPANISH FOOT A ribbed scroll foot typical of the William and Mary period; so-called because of Spanish-Portuguese designs and motifs introduced into Restoration England by Charles II's marriage to Catherine of Braganza

Spanish colonial chair

SPATTERWARE A cheerful Staffordshire export pottery made for provincial American trade, from about 1820 to 1860, the sponged or spattered patterns in lively designs

Spanish foot

SPICE CHEST Small cabinets lined with drawers in which precious imported spices could be locked up, 17th and 18th centuries; designed either to hang on the wall or stand on a table, with later examples often mounted on

Chippendale spider-leg table

Queen Anne splat-back chair

legs giving such spice chests the appearance of miniature highboys.

SPIDER An early name for a cast-iron frying pan, originally made with spiderlike legs to stand over the open coals in a fireplace

SPIDER-LEG TABLE A small, lightweight, gate-leg table, the legs slender and delicate; introduced from England in the Chippendale period

SPINDLE A thin rod, straight, tapered, or shaped with decorative turnings, primarily used as uprights in the back of a chair. See TURNINGS for illustrations

SPIRAL TURNING A decorative turning in a continuous twist or spiral. See TURNINGS for illustration

SPITTOON A receptacle for the convenience of spitters and tobacco chewers; a word coined in America early in the 1800's. While certain 18th-century French spittoons were of faïence or porcelain, the ubiquitous American spittoon, or cuspidor, was typically brass or of such ceramic ware as Bennington. Some were camouflaged by elaborate wooden cases.

SPLAT The flat central upright in the back of a chair, either solid, as in the splats of Queen Anne chairs, or pierced, as in the splats of the Chippendale period

SPLINT A thin strip of wood. Woven splints, in lieu of rush seats, were a colonial device that persisted in rural areas. Splint wood was also shaped into round, lidded boxes (bandboxes, cheeseboxes, and the like) throughout the 19th century.

SPLIT SPINDLES Turned spindles split lengthwise and applied ornamentally to a flat surface, as on early colonial forms of Jacobean design, or used in chair backs, such as the bannister-back of the William and Mary period. Typically, the spindle rod was split, glued together, turned on a lathe, then separated into matching halves.

SPONGE-PAINTED FURNITURE A decorative technique, chiefly 19th-century American provincial, in which paint was "sponged" onto furniture to create a textured effect

SPOOL FURNITURE General term for spool-turned furniture of the Victorian era. See COTTAGE FURNITURE, ELIZABETHAN REVIVAL STYLE, HIRED MAN'S BED, JENNY LIND BED

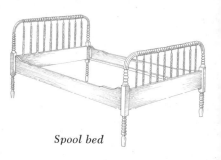

Spool bed

SPOOL TURNING Continuously repeated bulbous turning suggesting a row of spools. See TURNINGS

SPOON-BACK A chair back slightly curved to conform to the sitter's back; introduced in splat-back chairs of the Queen Anne period

SQUAB A removable cushion on the seat of a chair or sofa; introduced in the late 1600's, particularly for wooden or cane-seated chairs. The word squab is of ancient Scandinavian origin, meaning any object that is soft and fat.

SQUIRREL CAGE
See BIRD CAGE

S-SCROLL A scroll carved in the form of the letter S

STAFFORDSHIRE The English county known for its potteries, such as Spode, Wedgwood, Minton, and Copeland; now a general term for inexpensive

Squab on corner chair

wares imported to America, particularly from post-Revolutionary days on. Historic Staffordshire, for example, was designed for American trade with transfer-printed views of American notables, historical events, patriotic symbols, and American landscapes. Originally a rich cobalt blue on white, the early china is often known as "Old Blue." After 1830, sepia, green, lavender, black, and pink china was made. Ornamental bric-a-brac, often designed in pairs, was continuingly popular: trinket boxes, vases, little cottages and castles, historical and literary figurines, dogs, sheep, and deer, to name but a few.

Standing salt

STANDING SALT   A salt dish of impressive proportions, introduced in the Middle Ages; the tradition continued in early colonial America in the standing salts made by local silversmiths. The knobs, typically found on the rim of this type of dish, served to hold a napkin or plate as a cover for the precious salt, then an import.

STANDISH   A desk stand for writing accessories; early examples typically included an inkpot, a wafer box for wax sealing wafers, and a pounce box from which a fine powder (or pounce) was shaken over wet ink to prevent its spreading on unsized paper. Further elaborations included taper jacks, penknives (for sharpening quill pens), a small drawer, or a letter rack.

STATUARY WARE
See **PARIAN WARE**

Gothic Revival steeple clock

STEEPLE CLOCK   A Connecticut shelf clock with pointed top and pillars terminating in pointed finials, introduced about 1845 and made in many sizes and varieties; also called Gothic clock

STENCIL A painted or gilded design created with cutout patterns of paper or metal; an important decorative adjunct on mass-produced furniture, such as the Hitchcock chair. Stenciled patterns on plaster walls were an early American substitute for wallpaper. Stenciled tinware, from the late 1700's to the late 1800's, was widely produced both by professionals and amateurs.

STERLING A term applied to the English standard of silverware indicating a proportion of 925 parts fine silver and 75 parts fine copper in each 1000 parts, a standard comparable to that established by Edward I in 1300. A suggested derivation of the word is the little stars, or "star-lings," on early Norman coins. American silver was rarely stamped as sterling until the mid 1800's. See also HALLMARK

STICK BACK Colloquial name for spindled furniture, such as the Windsor chair; also called stick furniture

STICKLEY, GUSTAV (1857–1942) The Wisconsin-born designer and furniture maker, who initiated the so-called Mission style. Stickley's designs, which he called Craftsman furniture, were rectangular, unadorned, highly functional forms, principally in oak; they were his idealistic interpretation of the concepts developed in the English Arts and Crafts movement. First exhibited at a Grand Rapids furniture fair in 1900, Stickley's patterns were immediately copied and mass produced throughout the country, as well as lending themselves to homemade cabinetwork. Stickley produced his furniture from 1901 to his bankruptcy in 1915 at the Craftsman Workshops

Stickley Craftsman table

Stiegel-type
daisy-in-diamond bottle

near Syracuse, New York. See also MISSION STYLE and ROYCROFT SHOPS

STIEGEL, HENRY WILLIAM (1729–85) German-born iron and glass manufacturer of southeastern Pennsylvania. Among products made by his flourishing foundries were cast-iron stoves, frequently decorated with traditional Germanic patterns. In Manheim, the town which he established, Stiegel's glass factory was staffed by artisans imported from abroad. From 1765 until its financial failure in 1775, Stiegel produced a fine flint glass known for its deep shades of blue and purple, molded glass with ribbed, swirled, and quilted patterns (such as the daisy-in-diamond), and glass decorated with engravings or brightly enameled folk motifs. Because no identifying marks were used, it is almost impossible to determine with certainty those pieces made at Manheim. Further, Stiegel's glass influenced glassmakers who followed him. Therefore, the term Stiegel-type glass is used for those examples representative of his work. As for Stiegel himself, flamboyant, imprudent, and free-spending, he died an impoverished schoolmaster.

STILES The upright side supports of a chair back

STONEWARE A form of hard, nonporous pottery made of clay fired at high temperatures; often salt glazed. Typical of American production are the 19th-century crocks and jugs, frequently with cobalt blue underglaze decorations, and sometimes with sgraffito or ornaments in low relief.

STRAP HINGE A simple hinge with long leaves resembling straps; a pattern of ancient origin, widely used in

Stoneware crock

early American design and subsequent revival forms of a so-called medieval, colonial, or rustic nature

STRAPWORK Term for the designs created by applied split spindles and applied bosses used in America chiefly on such case pieces as the court cupboard of the 17th century; a modified version of elaborately carved bands and paneling introduced into Elizabethan England from the Continent during the Renaissance period

Strap hinge

STRAWBERRY-DIAMOND PATTERN On 19th-century pressed or cut glass, an allover pattern made up of diamonds enclosing smaller ones suggesting the shape of strawberries

STRETCHER A horizontal support bracing the legs of chairs, tables, stools, or case pieces

STRINGING In furniture, a line or thin band of wood used as an inlay set into a contrasting ground. Delicate stringing was a feature on Sheraton and Hepplewhite furniture. See BANDING for illustration

Stretcher-base table

STRIPED GLASS A thin glass striped in the Venetian manner with colored twists; also known as Lutz glass, after Nicholas Lutz, a French glassblower at the Boston & Sandwich Glass Company from 1869 to 1888, who worked in the Venetian tradition. Striped glass, however, was produced by other American glasshouses and is still being made to the present day.

STUDENT LAMP An adjustable kerosene desk lamp with one or two arms, typically of brass with a green glass shade; 1890 to 1915; sometimes known as a Harvard lamp

Student lamp

Suffolk latch,
Pennsylvania German

Swags on silver urn

Swing leg on Queen Anne table

STUMP LEG   A plain, square rear leg with a slight backward curve; in American cabinetwork typically used on chairs and sofas with front cabriole legs, such as certain Chippendale patterns and French revival styles of the Victorian period

SUFFOLK LATCH   A wrought-iron door handle and thumb latch, the design of medieval origin; made in America from the mid 1600's to the 1880's

SUGAR CHEST   A southern piece, usually made by plantation carpenter-cabinetmakers, about 1750–1860, in which sugar, spices, coffee, tea, and so forth were stored and locked; typically a standing chest on short legs, with one drawer below; inside the lift-top chest, various storage compartments

SUNFLOWER
See CONNECTICUT VALLEY SUNFLOWER CHEST

SURTOUT
See PLATEAU

SWAG   Swinging or suspended decoration, representing drapery, ribbons, garlands of fruit and flowers; also called festoon; a carved motif popular, for example, on furniture by Duncan Phyfe and his contemporaries

SWANNECK PEDIMENT
See SCROLL PEDIMENT

SWELL FRONT
See BOW FRONT

SWIFT   An adjustable reel for winding a hank of yarn into a ball; usually made of wood, but also found in ivory and in whalebone

SWING LEG   The leg that swings out to support a table leaf; popularized in the Queen Anne period; made without a supporting stretcher at the base, as were earlier gate-legs. See also GATE-LEG TABLE

SWIVEL CHAIR Chair with a revolving seat, rarely made before the 19th century. The adjustable swivel chair with springs was popularized in the mid 1800's; an 1851 model had bowed steel springs and an ornately scrolled and upholstered cast-iron frame. In 1853 Peter Ten Eyck patented an American swivel chair that was the future prototype—wooden construction, plain spindles across the back, curved steel rockers, a central pivot shaft, and four splayed legs joined underneath the seat to support the pivot. Spring-swivel chairs were originally designed as a type of rocker or easy chair for invalids, but were immediately adopted as office furnishings.

Tabernacle mirror

TABERNACLE MIRROR A gilded wall mirror, about 1795 to 1820, in the Sheraton style; a flat cornice with a row of gilt balls beneath it and applied columns on the sides of the frame; above the mirror section, a wood or glass panel with painted decoration, often on a patriotic theme

TABOURET
See DAMASCUS TABLE

TALL BOY
See CHEST-ON-CHEST

TALL CASE CLOCK A clock mounted in a tall, standing case; an English innovation, about 1660, designed to protect the works and the pendulum. (The pendulum was a Dutch invention, 1657–58.) Tall case clocks were made in America from the early 1700's on, in all varying contemporary styles. Also called a long case clock and a

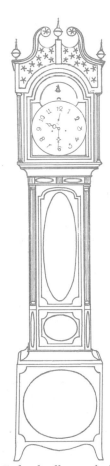

Federal tall case clock

Sheraton tambour desk

grandfather clock. See also GRAND-FATHER CLOCK

TAMBOUR A flexible sliding door made of thin strips of wood glued to a canvas backing; typically used on Hepplewhite and Sheraton style desks, either in a roll-top construction or as sliding horizontal doors. See also ROLL-TOP DESK

TAM O'SHANTER Popular name for glass shades used on kerosene lamps, because of their rounded resemblance to a tam o'shanter. Also known as umbrella shades. See STUDENT LAMP for illustration

TAPE LOOM A weaving device of ancient origin; a small, wooden, paddle-shaped hand loom, the central portion cut through in narrow lines; used in early American handicrafts to weave narrow strips of ribbon, trimming, or lace

TAPER JACK As introduced in England around 1700, a desk accessory designed to provide a small flame for melting the wax used to seal letters and documents. A spindle device holds a coil of taper (or waxed wick), the end of the taper threaded upward through a small armature that holds it in place when lit; made in silver and other metals. See also STANDISH

TAVERN TABLE A low, sturdy, rectangular table of Jacobean origin, popularly used in colonial taverns and public meeting houses; turned legs and stretchers; sometimes with a single drawer. Tavern tables, continued to be made in rural areas, roughly from the late 1700's to about 1830, usually without turnings on the legs or stretchers.

Tavern table

TEAKETTLE STAND A small elegant stand designed to hold a silver tea-kettle, or urn, with its spirit lamp; introduced in America in the Chippendale period, chiefly made in Hepplewhite and Sheraton styles. The top, occasionally made of marble, has a fretwork rim; below, a pull-out slide on which to rest the teapot while refilling it with hot water.

TEA LEAF A light, ironstone china decorated with copper or gold luster "tea leaf" sprigs, popular in the 1860's and 1870's, both as an English import and in domestic manufacture

TEARDROP HANDLE
See PEAR-DROP HANDLE

Queen Anne tea table

TEA TABLE An innovation of the late 17th century prompted by the wide popularity of tea, the newly introduced beverage from the Far East. In American cabinetwork, the tea table became prevalent in the Queen Anne period and reached fashionable heights during the Chippendale period. See also PEMBROKE TABLE and TILT-TOP TABLE

TENT BED
See FIELD BED

TENON
See MORTISE AND TENON

TESTER The canopy covering a high-post bed, from an early English word meaning a head covering or helmet. Beds with canopies of wood or fabric were an established European and English form. In early colonial America, canopy beds were extremely simple, the drapery often suspended from the ceiling. The first formal, sophisticated examples were produced in the Queen Anne period.

Tester on Empire bed

TÊTE-À-TÊTE
See CONVERSATIONAL

THEOREM PAINTING Paintings, usually on velvet, created with stencils; from about 1810 to 1840, a popular artistic pursuit for young ladies, with still-life compositions of fruits and flowers the most popular theme

THONET FURNITURE
See BENTWOOD FURNITURE

THUMBPRINT
See ARGUS

TIDY
See ANTIMACASSAR

TIEBACK As introduced from England in the mid 1700's, the early American tiebacks were either flat, gilded metal holders or rosettes, of metal or glass; continuingly made in varying contemporary styles and in such diverse materials as Sheffield plate, japanned tinware, papier-mâché, and carved wood. Also known as a curtain holder or curtain pin

TIFFANY, LOUIS COMFORT (1848–1933) Painter, designer, and decorator, the son of jeweler Charles Lewis Tiffany; the leading exponent of the Art Nouveau style in America. Tiffany's successful interior decorating firm, established in 1879, became secondary to his interest in stained glass and mosaics. Working with a staff of expert artisans, he developed a type of iridescent glass known as Favrile, and at the Tiffany Studios, founded in 1900, he designed and produced not only the Art Nouveau glassware for which he is famous, but bronze, ceramic, and enamel objects, from pen wipers to lighting fixtures, as well as art jewelry. See also PEACOCK MOTIF and FAVRILE

Tiffany wisteria lamp

TILT-TOP TABLE A table, usually mounted on tripod feet, the top hinged to tip to a vertical position; a device used from medieval times that reached its fullest and most elegant development in the late 18th century with the tilt-top tables of the Chippendale period. See also PIECRUST TABLE

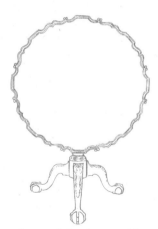

Chippendale tilt-top table

TINTYPE A photograph on a thin, black-japanned, iron plate, made by a collodion process; introduced in the 1860's and continuingly popular as a postcard-sized photo taken at resorts and carnivals by street photographers; also called a ferrotype

TINWARE Articles made from thin rolled sheets of tin-plated iron. Pre-Revolutionary tinware, limited by Britain's control of the tinware market, was usually plain and functional in design: sconces, cookie cutters, candlemolds, milk strainers, lanterns, funnels, and tinderboxes. Following the Revolution, American tinware flourished. Brightly painted or japanned pieces were highly popular to about 1860 in gay, unsophisticated patterns of flowers, fruits, running borders, birds, and gilt or bronzed stenciled motifs on trays, coffee and teapots, boxes of all kinds, salt and pepper shakers, tea caddies, and so forth. Also popular, among the Pennsylvania Germans in particular, were punched, pierced, and engraved tinwares. Japanned tinware is sometimes called Pontypool, after the British manufacturing center where japanned tin was widely produced and exported from about 1720. The most popular name for tinware, however, is tôle — from the extensive and fashionable French imports of the Empire period. See also TÔLE

Tôle coffeepot

TOBY JUG A figure mug or jug, first made in England in the mid 1700's. The figure, wearing a three-cornered hat, represented Toby Phillpot, the toper, subject of a popular song, "The Brown Jug." Toby jugs and bottles, whether of Toby or of other figures, were made at American potteries from the early 1800's on.

TOILET GLASS
See DRESSING GLASS

TOILETTINETTE A lady's toilet table of the Victorian period

TÔLE An abbreviation of *tôle peinte*, the French term for painted sheet iron, used decoratively—as in jardinieres and in shades for candlesticks; popular in the French Empire period. Now, tôle is a general term for painted tinware.

TORUS A bold, semicircular, convex molding. See MOLDINGS for illustration

TOWNSEND
See GODDARD AND TOWNSEND

TRACERY Originally, the delicate decorative openwork in Gothic windows; then copied by wood carvers as an ornamental detail, either solid or pierced. In the Gothic Revival style, for example, chair backs were carved in tracery patterns.

TRAMMEL A pothook, adjusted by ratchets, to be hung from a crane in a fireplace; used in colonial America and in rural areas through the 19th century; also a similar device for raising and lowering lamps

TRANSFER PRINTING
See PRINTED WARE

TRANSITIONAL The general term for

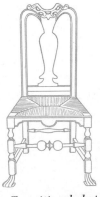

Transitional chair

any article of furniture that combines patterns of an earlier style with a newly fashionable style

TREEN Meaning "made of tree"; hand-turned, wooden, domestic objects, such as bowls, mugs, spoons, trenchers, mortars and pestles, and other kitchen utensils; an Old World tradition continued in America well into the 19th century

TREE OF LIFE A decorative motif originating in oriental and Sanskrit mythology; a stylized tree growing from a vase introduced to the Western world in the 17th century; popular, for example, in early crewelwork patterns, and depicted as the Tree of Life from the Garden of Eden in Pennsylvania German decorative motifs, as well as in the inspirational drawings of heavenly vistas done by the Shakers

TREFOIL A stylized, three-lobed design, often used in Gothic and Gothic Revival patterns

Trefoil

TRENCHER A flat wooden plate or platter used throughout the colonial years and into the 1800's in rural districts. The word is derived from the French *tranche,* a thick cut of bread, which served as a plate in the Middle Ages.

TRESTLE TABLE A table with trestles as the supporting framework, an outgrowth of medieval dining tables which were merely loose boards resting on trestles. Fixed trestle tables became commonplace early in the 1500's, the basic form reproduced in early colonial America, particularly in English settlements, and continuingly made throughout the country in provincial styles. See also SAWBUCK TABLE

Trestle table

Trifid foot

TRIANGLE CHAIR
See HARVARD CHAIR

TRIFID FOOT A three-toed foot; particularly associated with Queen Anne cabinetwork; sometimes known as a drake foot or web foot

TRIPOD TABLE Any table supported by three legs; in American cabinetwork, a general term for a small, incidental table supported on a central shaft with three outflaring feet, usually with a tilt-top; a favorite pattern of the Chippendale period. See also CANDLE-STAND, PIE-CRUST TABLE, TEA TABLE, and TILT-TOP TABLE

TRIVET A decorative metal stand with three short legs used on the hearth or table to support hot objects, such as a kettle, plate, or flatiron

TRUMPET TURNING A turned leg that has the profile of an upturned trumpet; a William and Mary design. See TURNINGS for illustration

TRUNDLE BED A low bed on wheels, usually for a child; designed to be trundled or rolled under a large bed when not in use; of late medieval origin, made in America into the 19th century. Also called a truckle bed

TUCKAWAY TABLE An early colonial version, about 1690 to 1710, of a small, compact English gate-leg table; typically made with a pair of crossed gate-legs that close flat and a round top that folds down. The table then can be tucked away until needed.

TUCKER PORCELAIN The earliest successful commercial American porcelain, made from 1825 to 1838 at the Philadelphia pottery established by William Ellis Tucker. In imitation of

Tucker porcelain teapot

Sèvres designs, much of the porcelain was ornamented with delicate floral patterns and gilt trim. Other decoration included American landscapes or historical portraits and emblems, often in sepia.

TULIP MOTIF In the decorative arts, a stylized tulip; popularized in Europe in the 16th century with the introduction of tulips from the Near East; used as a carved or painted motif on chests in Holland, Germany, England, and subsequently in early America. Particularly favored among Pennsylvania Germans. The tulip motif was so widely reproduced on Pennsylvania German pottery that it became known as tulip ware. In 19th-century America, a three-lobed tuliplike pattern was used on various pressed glass. See also CONNECTICUT VALLEY SUNFLOWER CHEST and IPSWICH CHEST

Tulip motif on
Pennsylvania German chest

TUMBLER A drinking glass without a foot or stem. The name derived from a medieval glass with a pointed end that could not be set down until empty, because it would tumble and spill.

TURKEY RED A rich shade of red, the dye introduced from the Near East and made from madder, a Eurasian herb; a popular color in Victorian cotton fabrics. Family dining tables across the country were covered with turkey red cotton damask cloths, both of European and American manufacture, with woven white patterns, including the Greek key, flowers, fruits, birds, and medallions, either bought finished or by the yard at such stores as Sears, Roebuck and Company, from 1878, or Woolworth's, from 1879.

TURKEY WORK A type of needlework,

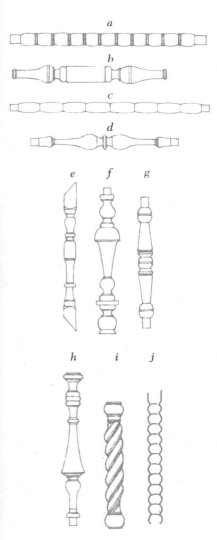

Turnings: (a) Ball-and-ring. (b) Block-and-vase. (c) Sausage. (d) Vase-and-ring. (e) Baluster. (f) Cup. (g) Spindle. (h) Trumpet. (i) Spiral. (j) Spool

popularized in late 16th-century England, imitative of the pile carpets imported from the East. Turkey work, for cushions, upholstery, and table coverings, was used in 17th-century America.

TURKISH CORNER In the late 19th century, an informal alcove or corner of a room for lolling and smoking, heavily upholstered and furnished in a manner to evoke Near Eastern *décor;* also called a cozy corner

TURKISH STYLE The late Victorian *décor* and furnishings inspired by Near Eastern exhibits at the Philadelphia Centennial Exhibition, 1876; also defined as the Moorish style. Rooms were decorated with Moorish arches, wallpapers in oriental patterns, Near Eastern metalwork, such as pierced hanging lamps, brass trays, temple bells, and so forth, imported, inlaid Near Eastern furniture, such as the tabouret or Damascus table. Overstuffed furniture, usually tufted and fringed, was manufactured in imitation of Turkish modes, and oriental motifs were incorporated into cabinetwork. See also DAMASCUS TABLE, DIVAN, OTTOMAN, and TURKISH CORNER

TURNING An ancient woodworking process, in which pieces of wood are symmetrically cut or shaped while turning on a lathe; typically used for shaping legs, posts, spindles, feet, rungs, and stretchers. In English cabinetwork, turnery was first widely used in the 16th century.

TURNIP FOOT A variation of the ball foot, having a collar or footing at the bottom; William and Mary period

TWIN BEDS A pair of matching single

beds; Sheraton's *Drawing-Book* (1790) offered a twin bed design called a Summer Bed, "intended for a nobleman or gentleman and his lady to sleep in separately in hot weather." Twin beds, however, were not prevalent until the 1890's when they were popularized by the manufacturers of brass and cast-iron bedsteads.

VASA MURRHINA   A "metallized" transparent art glass, the effect of gold and silver flecks created by flakes of mica suspended within the glass; made from about 1880 to 1910 in imitation of ancient Roman vessels carved from murra, a semiprecious stone

VASE TURNING   A turning resembling a vase with a taper above a bulbous base; introduced in William and Mary patterns. See TURNINGS (b, d) for illustration

VENEER   A thin sheet of wood applied to a solid surface; an exacting decorative technique, using exotic and richly figured woods, introduced from Holland to Restoration England; used in America on furniture of the William and Mary period, and revived as an elegant ornamental feature of Hepplewhite and Sheraton patterns. Machine-made and mass-produced veneered furniture in the Victorian era gave rise to the popular but mistaken idea of veneer being a cheap imitative process.

Veneered William and Mary desk

VERRE ÉGLOMISÉ   The French term for glass painted and ornamented on the underside and used as decorative inserts in cabinetwork; an ornamental motif popular in the Federal period. The word *églomisé* came from the name of an 18th-century French framer and designer, Jean-Baptiste Glomi.

VICTORIAN PERIOD The years of Queen Victoria's reign, 1837 to 1901, in which furniture design is roughly divided into three broad categories: Early Victorian, 1837–50; Mid-Victorian, 1850–80; and Late Victorian, 1880–1901. Decorative arts throughout the entire era were characterized by the borrowing and mingling of assorted past styles and motifs, as well as adaptations from Near Eastern and oriental patterns.

VOLUTE A scroll-like conformation used in classical capitals, especially of the Ionic order. See CLASSICAL ORDER

WAFER BOX See STANDISH

WAGON SEAT A low, sturdy, wooden settee, typically with a splat back; about 1780 to 1850; used both in the house and in the back of a wagon as extra seating. Also known as a rumble seat, because it was in the rear over the rumbling wheels

WAG ON THE WALL The popular name for any early wall clock with the weights and pendulum left uncovered. Up to about 1825, the dial and works intended for tall case clocks were often bought separately and hung directly on the wall.

WAINSCOT CHAIR A wooden armchair with a paneled back, specifically in the Jacobean style reproduced in 17th-century America. The word wainscot is derived from a Dutch word for a type of oaken plank used in the Middle Ages for the construction of wagons [or wains]; the word then came into use for oaken wall paneling, and by extension, to paneled chairs.

WALL POCKET A catchall device of

Wainscot chair

the Victorian era, hung upon the wall to hold any number of objects, from newspapers and letters to sewing equipment and whisk brooms; typically in ornate needlework, beadwork, and jig-saw work

WARMING PAN A long-handled covered pan that held hot coals; an early device for warming cold sheets and bedding before the household retired; typically of brass, with a decorative pierced design in the cover of the pan, and a turned wooden handle

Warming pan

WATER BENCH A kitchen piece particularly favored among the Pennsylvania Germans, from about 1800 to 1870; a type of dresser with an open counter to hold buckets of fresh water and cupboards below for pitchers, extra buckets, dippers, and so forth. Also known as a bucket bench

WATER LEAF An ornamental detail of classical origin; delicate, elongated leaves in a repetitive pattern, popular in carvings on Hepplewhite and Sheraton furniture, and particularly used by Duncan Phyfe as a decorative motif on legs and pedestals

WEB FOOT
See TRIFID FOOT

WEDGWOOD Chinaware produced at the Staffordshire pottery founded by Josiah Wedgwood in 1759, extensively exported to America from that date to the present day. Among early exports were salt-glazed stoneware, cauliflower ware, Queen's Ware (or creamware, perfected by Wedgwood), blue jasper ware with white cameolike decorations in relief, and the transfer-printed wares with American historic and scenic motifs. See also STAF-

WELLS FARGO DESK
See WOOTEN'S PATENT DESK

WELSH DRESSER Popular name for a provincial dresser or sideboard, of a type with a ceiling-high set of open shelves above, drawers and occasionally cupboards below, and often with trim sawn in scalloped patterns; a traditional form in rural England, of Jacobean origin, and particularly associated in America with the Welsh colonists who settled in Pennsylvania

WESTWARD HO A pressed-glass pattern, originally called Pioneer, inspired by the Centennial celebrations of 1876 and decorated with western motifs: running bison and deer, a log cabin in the mountains, and handles in the shape of Indians on the covers of such items as butter dishes and compotes

Whale-oil lamp, pressed-glass

WHALE-OIL LAMP Lamp designed to burn whale oil, a cheap, clean, popular fuel. Whale-oil lamps were produced from about 1787 until after the Civil War in various materials—tin, brass, pewter, pressed glass—and fitted with one or two round wicks. A variation, the peg lamp, used early in the 1800's, consisted of a burner and font with a stubby peg that fit into a candlestick socket, thereby converting the candlestick into a whale-oil lamp.

WHATNOT A set of open shelves, either standing or hung on the wall, for the display of bric-a-brac; popularized early in the 1800's, to become a favorite piece of furniture during the Victorian era. Also called an étagère, the 17th-century French term for decorative open shelves

Victorian whatnot

WHEAT MOTIF A decorative motif, such as the wheat ears carved on chair-back patterns of the Hepplewhite period, and the bound sheaves of wheat, sometimes with a sickle, on the handles of knives, forks, and spoons of the Empire period; also a popular motif in pressed glass. The term wheat sheaf back is a latter-day descriptive phrase for chairs with pierced splat or spindle designs resembling a stylized sheaf, bound at the "waist" and fanning out above and below to join the cresting and the chair seat; a pattern variously used, for example, in chairs of the Chippendale period.

Wheat motif

WHIMSEY Term for odd or unusual pieces of glass, such as hats, horns, slippers, rolling pins, made by glass blowers as gifts for family and friends. Whimsey is also used occasionally for the pressed-glass novelties so popular in the mid- and late-Victorian era, such as little boots to hold matches or little fans to use as butter dishes.

WHITE ON WHITE The popular name for white quilts elaborately patterned with white stitching; a form of quilting brought from England and Europe by the early colonial settlers. See also PATCHWORK QUILT

WHORL FOOT A Chippendale foot consisting of an upturned scroll; also called a knurl foot or French scroll foot

Whorl foot

WICKERWORK Furniture and other forms woven from willow twigs, an age-old technique that became fashionable after the Civil War for garden and porch furniture, as well as for light, decorative interior furnishings

WILLIAM AND MARY STYLE (1685–1720) A furniture style named for the

William and Mary highboy

European patterns of baroque inspiration brought from Holland to England during William and Mary's reign, 1689–1702. In America the William and Mary style marked a distinct break from the medieval heritage expressed in the earlier massive forms of the Jacobean period. The new style was one of elegance, lighter proportions, and fine carving in such motifs as C- and S-scrolls, Spanish feet, arched and serpentine stretchers, and pierced crestings on chairs and mirrors. The use of fine-grained woods, particularly walnut, was emphasized; veneer, japanning, and woven cane (for seats and back panels) were introduced, as were such new forms as the highboy, the lowboy, the day bed, the easy chair, and the gate-leg table. See also RESTORATION CHAIR

WILLOW MOUNTS Escutcheons for drawer handles used during the Chippendale period; basically shaped like the earlier bat's-wing mounts but with a far more elaborate, baroque outline. The source of the name is unknown. See ESCUTCHEON

WILLOW WARE A deep blue and white transfer-printed chinaware in the oriental mode, originally designed in England around 1780 by Thomas Minton; probably the most popular of chinaware patterns in America, and still being produced today, even on paper plates. The pattern shows an oriental landscape with pagodas, trees, a little bridge crossed by three small figures, and two birds in the sky. The design was explained by a story of star-crossed lovers pursued by the maiden's irate father, the lovers' souls transformed after death into birds. Minton's willow pattern was quickly

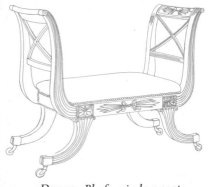

Duncan Phyfe window seat

adopted by potteries in France, Germany, America, and even in the Orient —where it was copied as an inexpensive export for the Western world.

WINDOW SEAT A bench, either upholstered or caned, with two ends or "arms"; designed to fit in a window recess; popularized through 18th-century English patterns

WINDSOR CHAIRS Also originally known as stick chairs, their basic construction being a plank seat with stick legs and stick spindles; an age-old technique, first widely produced in 17th-century England as cottage furniture and presumably named for the market town of Windsor. This type of chair appeared in America early in the 1700's and became immediately popular throughout the colonies; typically with turned, splayed legs and frequently painted, with green the favorite color. The initial form was the low-back Windsor, now often known as a firehouse chair or captain's chair, to be followed by the comb-back, the bow-back, the fan-back, the arch-back (a continuous hoop-and-arm design), and a host of variations from settees to high chairs. Stylized bamboo-turned legs were introduced around 1790. Arrow-back Windsors, made with flat, arrow-shaped spindles and generally painted black with gold details, were popular throughout the early 1800's. See also ROCKING BENCH and SADDLE SEAT

WING CHAIR Popular name for the upholstered easy chair with wing-shaped sidings that jut forward at head level from the back of the chair; a pattern designed to cut down drafts that was introduced late in the 17th century. See also EASY CHAIR

Windsor chairs:

Low-back

Hoop-back

Comb-back

Brace-back

WINTHROP DESK The popular but mistaken name for a Chippendale slant-top desk that came into fashion in the mid 1700's. The Winthrop name has no basis in fact; the three John Winthrops who were early colonial governors lived well before Chippendale fashions were introduced in America. Also known as a Governor Winthrop desk

Wistar-type glass bowl

WISTAR, CASPAR (Died 1752) German-born glassmaker, whose factory— founded in Salem County, New Jersey, in 1739—was the first successful American glasshouse. Beside the standard output of bottles, window glass, and other household articles, the factory is credited with the development of the so-called New Jersey style of glass, characterized by the lily-pad pattern and by thin threading around the necks of such forms as pitchers. Upon Wistar's death, the factory was directed by his son until 1780. See also SOUTH JERSEY GLASS and LILY PAD

WITCH BALL A hollow ball of glass, free-blown in various colors, often with white loopings; a novelty glass or whimsey made until the closing years of the 19th century. According to legend, which may or may not have a basis in fact, clusters of glass balls were once hung overhead to warn against witches on the wing. In the Victorian era, however, witch balls were used as ornaments (heaped in a bowl, for example) or served as covers for wide-mouthed pitchers.

WOODEN INDIAN
See CIGAR-STORE INDIAN

WOODENWARE
See TREEN

WOOTEN'S PATENT DESK A monumental, six-feet-tall, paneled desk patented in 1874 by W. S. Wooten and constructed to serve as an entire office, complete with a letter slot. When closed, the desk resembled a large cupboard, the front rounding off at the top. The hinged front sections opened in the middle and swung out to each side, the interior fitted with innumerable pigeon holes, shelves, drawers, and a fall-front writing surface. This type of office-in-one is also known as a Wells Fargo desk.

WORK TABLE A small table fitted with accessories for needlework, often made with one or two drawers, and frequently with a suspended fabric workbag. The work table, which became fashionable and prevalent in the mid 1700's, evolved from the earlier sewing box and continued as elegantly designed cabinetwork in various contemporary styles. See also MARTHA WASHINGTON TABLE

YELLOW WARE The name often given to creamware or Queen's Ware; also the term sometimes used for a canary yellow ware decorated with bright provincial designs that was one of the English "gaudy ware" imports so popular in rural America during the late 1700's and early 1800's.

ZOAR A German religious community, founded in 1817 in Ohio. Like the Pennsylvania Germans, the Zoar settlers reproduced the folk patterns of their homeland, such as the plank chair, and used the traditional decorative motifs, such as hearts, painted birds and flowers, and simple punchwork designs on wood.

Sheraton work table

Benⁿ Randolph
Cabinet Maker
at the Golden Eagle in Chesnut Street
—— Between third and fourth Streets, ——
PHILADELPHIA,
Makes all Sorts of Cabinet & Chair work
Likewise Carving Gilding &c Perform'd in the Chinese
and Modern Tastes

Style
Charts

The Jacobean Style

A distinctly medieval flavor is reflected in the first furniture made in colonial America. These 17th-century patterns, brought from the Old World, were the furniture forms that had evolved over past centuries in England and northern Europe, to remain more or less unchanged from the 1400's on—except, of course, for refinements in workmanship and in increasingly elaborate ornamental detail.

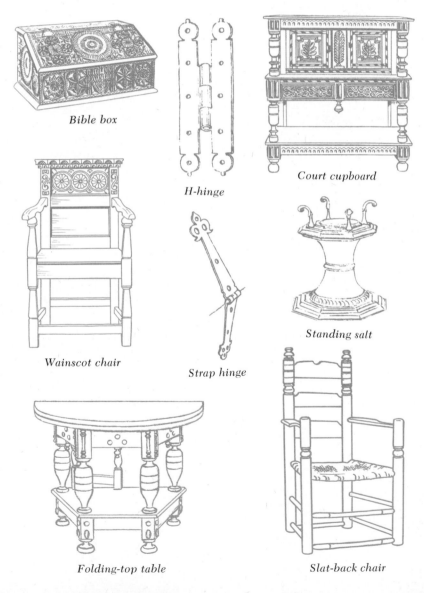

Bible box

H-hinge

Court cupboard

Wainscot chair

Strap hinge

Standing salt

Folding-top table

Slat-back chair

Carver chair

Brewster chair

Joint stool

Ipswich chest

Stretcher-base table

Trestle table

Connecticut Valley sunflower chest

Chair-table

The William and Mary Style

These patterns (1685–1720) mark the break with the medieval past. The new elegance was essentially European baroque, very leggy in feeling with much emphasis on ornamental stretchers — the X-shaped stretcher, hooped and scrolled stretchers, and so forth. Europe's trade with the East had introduced such oriental overtones as caned seating and japanned surfaces in imitation of imported lacquer.

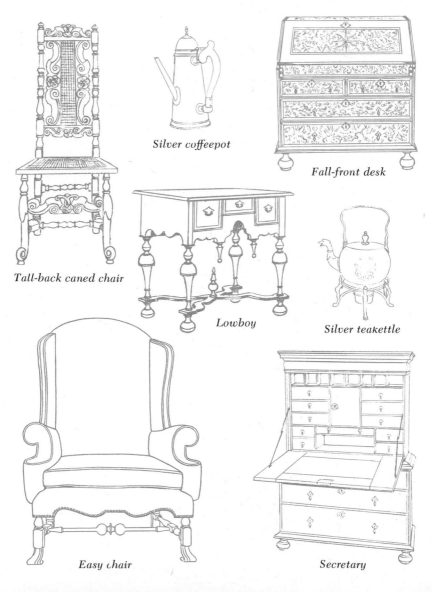

Silver coffeepot

Fall-front desk

Tall-back caned chair

Lowboy

Silver teakettle

Easy chair

Secretary

Boston chair   *Secretary*   *Banister-back chair*

Silver sugar bowl

Flemish-scroll day bed   *Splay-leg table*

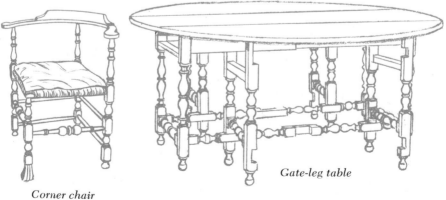

Corner chair   *Gate-leg table*

The Queen Anne Style

A simplified but sophisticated outgrowth of William and Mary designs, Queen Anne (1720–50) was an English version of the new rococo patterns of the French court. Curves were the focal point—on cabriole legs, in the shape of chair backs, in ornamental details. Classical motifs were a further enhancement: scallop shells, urns, the acanthus, and on case pieces, the architectural pediment.

Fall-front desk

Drop-leaf table

Silver cream pitcher

Secretary

Lowboy

Silver teapot

Easy chair

Fiddle-back chair

Highboy

Gaming table

Silver coffeepot

Silver cream pitcher

Tea table

Silver salt

Splat-back chair

Corner chair

Settee

The Chippendale Style

This richly ornamented, solid furniture (1750–85) was the culmination of the Georgian view of French rococo. Chippendale's name was a latter-day title, his talents as a designer having been recognized through his furniture manuals, which pictured such decorative motifs as Chinese fretwork, Gothic traceries in openwork carving on chair backs, and the straight, square, Marlborough leg.

Bombé secretary

Settee

Lowboy

Silver teakettle

Tilt-top table

Silver cream pitcher

Upholstered armchair

Chest-on-chest

Drop-leaf dining table

Silver coffeepot

Spider-leg table

Highboy

Pierced-splat chair

Card table

Tea table

The Federal Style

In a complete turnabout from the solidity of Chippendale forms came the delicate grace of the classical revival patterns (1783–1815), popularized in England by the Adams brothers and widely circulated by Sheraton and Hepplewhite pattern books. In America, since this period began at the close of the colonial era, classical revival furniture and architecture is popularly called the Federal style.

Hepplewhite sideboard

Gilt looking glass

Tilt-top candlestand

Sheraton dressing bureau

Silver sugar urn

Sheraton tambour desk

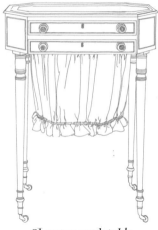

Sheraton work table

Cut-glass goblet

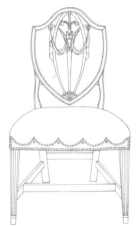

Hepplewhite shield-back chair

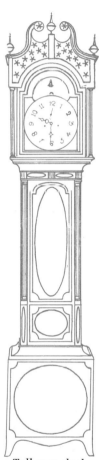

Tall case clock

Duncan Phyfe sofa

Sheraton card table

Silver and glass Argand lamp

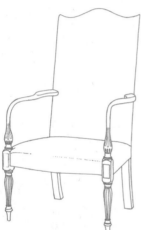

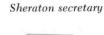

Sheraton secretary

Martha Washington chair

Banjo clock

Hepplewhite chest of drawers

*Sheraton square-
back chair*

The Empire Style

These majestic patterns, a further step in the neoclassic furniture inspired by Greek, Roman, and Egyptian antiquities, were created by Napoleon's designers and decorators to fulfill the Emperor's dreams of splendor. American versions (1815–40) of the Empire style ranged from extravagant grandeur to highly simplified forms that lent themselves to mass production toward mid-century.

Récamier-style sofa

Silver, anthemion motif

Tucker porcelain coffeepot

Klismos chair

Duncan Phyfe window seat

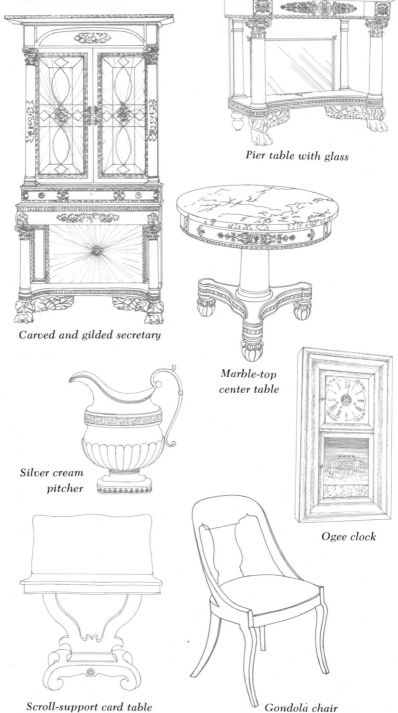

Pier table with glass

Carved and gilded secretary

Marble-top
center table

Silver cream
pitcher

Ogee clock

Scroll-support card table

Gondola chair

Work table on pedestal

Cut-glass compote

Lyre-back armchair

Card table with eagle supports

Tabernacle mirror

Four-poster bed

Early Victorian Styles

The Victorian period, which began in America roughly about 1840, was marked with a flurry of revival forms—Gothic, Elizabethan, Baroque or Louis XIV, Rococo or Louis XV, and an overall eclectic mélange of past styles that created, in effect, the new Victorian style. Fresh techniques and materials were also explored, resulting in such innovations as the bent-metal rocking chair, made around 1850.

Cast-iron mirror   Rococo Revival whatnot   Silver sugar bowl

Rococo Revival dressing table   Astral lamp   Rococo Revival chair

Gothic Revival steeple clock

Bohemian ruby-
glass compote

Gothic Revival chair

Eclectic chair

Elizabethan Revival
dressing table

Balloon-back chair

Eclectic gaming table
Metal-frame rocker

The Renaissance Revival Style

This ornate style, yet another Victorian version of past fashions, originated in France where court designers were kept busy redecorating royal palaces for Napoleon III and his empress, Eugénie. Her fondness for overstuffed furniture also prompted the lavish use of upholstery. Popular in America from about 1850 to 1875, simplified Renaissance forms were mass produced in factories throughout the country.

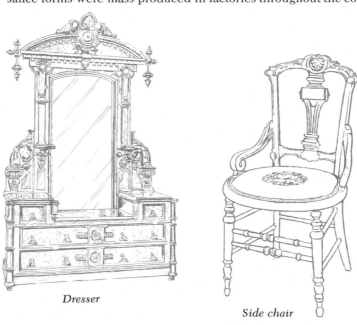

Dresser

Side chair

Bureau

Inlaid table

Sofa

Hallstand

Upholstered armchair

Side table

Bed

Armchair

The Eastlake Style

Charles Eastlake's concept of medieval simplicity was an instant success both in England and America upon publication of *Hints on Household Taste*, 1868. (The chair shown on top of page 179 is one of his original designs.) While some cabinetmakers did indeed emulate Eastlake's creed of simplicity, the Victorian world interpreted his patterns, by and large, in typically overblown Victorian terms.

Platform rocker

Cabinet organ

Bureau

Cupboard

Upholstered armchair

"Bamboo" rocker

Bed

Mid- and Late-Victorian Styles

There was apparently no limit to revival styles, new materials, and new mixtures of techniques and designs. In short, this was an era (mid-century to about 1900) in which a hodgepodge of patterns was drawn from innumerable sources — bamboo designs from the Orient, upholstered seating from Turkey, horn furniture from the Golden West, and cast-iron garden benches imitative of French rococo.

Cast-iron garden bench

Glass "nesting hen"

Cottage dresser

Hunzinger chair

Morris chair

Colonial Revival dressing table

Simulated bamboo table

Rood music stand

Ottoman

Conversational

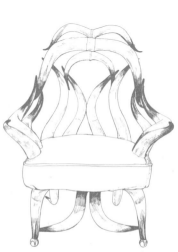

Steer-horn chair

Art Nouveau

An artistic rebellion against Victorian eclecticism and the stale revival of past patterns resulted in the Art Nouveau movement with designs based on undulating, flowering patterns drawn from natural forms. The style began in Europe in the late 1870's and became popular in America shortly thereafter, particularly in decorative arts such as graphics, metalwork, jewelry, glass, and so forth.

Silver hairbrush

Tiffany wisteria lamp

Tiffany Favrile peacock vase

Tiffany Peacock mirror

Side chair

Table by Edward Colonna

Silver paperknife

Bicycle poster by Will Bradley

*Silver and Favrile
glass candleholder*

Tiffany dragonfly lamp

Silver-deposit vase

Lily lamp

The Mission Style

This furniture, an American innovation introduced by Gustav Stickley in 1901 as Craftsman Furniture, was yet another effort to shake off Victorian furbelows and shams—what Eastlake and Art Nouveau designers had attempted earlier, each in their own way. Mission offered medieval, square-shaped, oaken forms that were solidly made in rugged, unpretentious patterns, utterly free of Victorian frills.

Sofa

Library table

Lamp

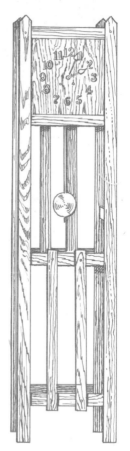

Standing clock　　　　　　　*Desk-bookcase*

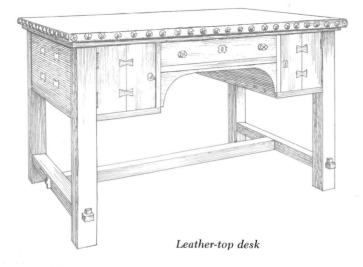

Leather-top desk

"Grand Rapids" Styles

Mail-order catalogues and inexpensive furniture stores at the turn of the century offered an almost limitless range of forms and fashions — generally in oak and often finished in the light color known as "golden" oak, which gave its name to these styles, as did the Grand Rapids factories that produced so much of this furniture. The bedstead, 1907, anticipates the plain and severe forms of the 1920's.

Parlor table

Oak desk-bookcase

Oak davenport-bed

Oak pedestal table

Clock-hallstand

Gumwood bed

Bibliography

GENERAL INFORMATION

Christensen, Erwin O. *The Index of American Design.* New York: The Macmillan Company, 1950.

Comstock, Helen, editor. *The Concise Encyclopedia of American Antiques.* Two volumes. New York: Hawthorne Books, Inc., 1957.

Davidson, Marshall B., author and editor. *The American Heritage History of Antiques.* Associate author and editor, Mary Durant. Three volumes. New York: American Heritage Publishing Co., Inc., 1967–69.

McClinton, Katherine Morrison. *Collecting American Victorian Antiques.* New York: Charles Scribner's Sons, 1966.

Shull, Thelma. *Victorian Antiques.* Rutland, Vermont: Charles E. Tuttle Co., Inc., 1963.

CHINAWARE AND POTTERY

Barret, Carter. *Bennington Pottery and Porcelain.* New York: Bonanza Books, © 1958.

Kovel, Ralph M., and Kovel, Terry H. *Dictionary of Marks — Pottery and Porcelain.* New York: Crown Publishing, Inc., © 1953.

Larsen, Ellouise Baker. *American Historical Views on Staffordshire China.* Second edition. New York: Doubleday & Company, Inc., 1950.

Mudge, Jean McClure. *Chinese Export Porcelain for American Trade, 1785–1835.* New York: University of Delaware Press, 1962.

FURNITURE

Andrews, Edward, and Andrews, Faith. *Shaker Furniture.* 1937. Reprint. New York: Dover Publications, Inc., 1950.

Bjerkoe, Ethel Hall. *The Cabinetmakers of America.* New York: Doubleday & Company, Inc., 1957.

Butler, Joseph T. *American Antiques, 1800–1900.* New York: Odyssey Press, 1965.

Comstock, Helen. *American Furniture.* New York: The Viking Press, Inc., 1962.

Downs, Joseph. *American Furniture, Queen Anne and Chippendale Periods.* New York: The Macmillan Company, 1952.

Kovel, Ralph M., and Kovel, Terry H., *American Country Furniture, 1780–1875.* New York: Crown Publishers, Inc., 1965.

Montgomery, Charles. *American Furniture of the Federal Period, 1788–1825.* New York: The Viking Press, Inc., 1966.

Nutting, Wallace. *Furniture Treasury.* New York: The Macmillan Company, 1954.

Ormsbee, Thomas H. *Field Guide to American Victorian Furniture*. Boston: Little, Brown and Company, 1952.
Ormsbee, Thomas H. *Field Guide to Early American Furniture*. Boston: Little, Brown and Company, 1951.
Otto, Celia Jackson. *American Furniture of the Nineteenth Century*. New York: The Viking Press, Inc., 1965.

GLASS

Lee, Ruth Webb. *Early American Pressed Glass*. Wellesley Hills, Massachusetts: Lee Publications, 1950.
McKearing, Helen, and McKearing, George S. *American Glass*. New York: Crown Publishers, Inc., 1948.
Revi, Albert C. *American Art Nouveau Glass*. Camden, New Jersey: Thomas Nelson & Sons, 1968.
Revi, Albert C. *Nineteenth Century Glass*. London: Thomas Nelson & Sons, 1967.

METALS

Kauffman, Henry J. *American Copper and Brass*. Camden, New Jersey: Thomas Nelson & Sons, 1968.
McClinton, Katherine Morrison. *Collecting American 19th Century Silver*. New York: Charles Scribner's Sons, 1968.
McLanathan, Richard, editor. *Colonial Silversmiths, Masters and Apprentices*. Boston: Museum of Fine Arts, 1956.
Powers, Beatrice Farnsworth, and Floyd, Olive. *Early American Decorated Tinware*. New York: Hastings House, Publishers, Inc., © 1957.
Rainwater, Dorothy T. *American Silver Manufacturers*. Hanover, Pennsylvania: Everybodys Press, © 1966.

MISCELLANEOUS SUGGESTIONS

Boyd, E. *Saints and Saint Makers*. Santa Fe, New Mexico: Laboratory of Anthropology, 1946.
Chippendale, Thomas. *The Gentleman and Cabinet-Maker's Director*. 1762. Reprint. New York: Dover Publications, Inc., 1962.
Eastlake, Charles L. *Hints on Household Taste*. 1878. Reprint. New York: Dover Publications, Inc., 1966.
Harbeson, Georgiana Brown. *American Needlework*. New York, Bonanza Books, © 1938.
Hayward, Arthur H. *Colonial Lighting*. Reprint. New York: Dover Publications, Inc., 1962.
Hepplewhite, George. *The Cabinet-Maker and Upholsterer's Guide*. 1762. Reprint. New York: Dover Publications, Inc., 1966.
Lichten, Frances M. *Decorative Art of Victoria's Era*. New York: Bonanza Books, 1950.
Lichten, Frances M. *Folk Art of Rural Pennsylvania*. New York: Charles Scribner's Sons, © 1946.
McClintock, Marshall, and McClintock, Inez. *Toys in America*. Washington, D.C: Public Affairs Press, 1961.
Palmer, Brooks. *The Book of American Clocks*. New York: The Macmillan Company, 1950.